DE BEERS

JEWELLERY

© De Beers Diamond Jewellers
© 2011 Assouline Publishing
601 West 26th Street, 18th floor
New York, NY 10001, USA
Tel.: 212 989 6810   Fax: 212 647 0005
www.assouline.com
Printed by Grafiche Milani S.p.a. (Italy).
ISBN: 9782759405107
No part of this book may be
reproduced in any form without
prior permission from the publisher.

De Beers Diamond Jewellers
45 Old Bond Street
London W1S 4QT, UK
Tel: +44 (0) 207 758 9750
www.debeers.com

CREDITS

DE BEERS

JEWELLERY

ASSOULINE

With over 120 years of
diamond expertise, De Beers Diamond
Jewellers was born from a legacy that is rich with
heritage and infused with legends of our iconic muse, the
diamond. At the heart of our designs is a melding of substance and
style; De Beers Diamond Jewellers brings together the diamond's dualities
of science and poetry, and unites its fascinating history and long traditions
with contemporary creativity and cutting-edge craftsmanship. The diamond
is a sparkling, celebratory symbol of continuity and eternity, of love and hope
for the future, and the De Beers goal is to bring this sublime symmetry to light in
our classically elegant jewellery. From the early myths surrounding diamonds
to their first discovery in India and the painstaking creation of timeless
modern-day treasures, this book is a journey that we invite you to take
with us. Placing our creative ethos in the context of contemporary art
from around the world, we explore both art in nature and the innate
beauty of creativity. By commissioning artists to work with us
on this path of articulating our identity, we have discovered
our own language, a voice that fuses contemporary life
with integrity, innovation and freedom. De Beers
presents to you this inspirational glimpse
at the home of the eternal diamond,
where both rough and polished
diamonds shine and
sparkle with the
light of
life.

The diamond occupies an astonishingly unique place in the story of civilisation. A dazzling fragment of eternity, it has shed its divine light through thousands of years, captivating mankind with its otherworldly beauty, engendering superstitions and supernatural beliefs, spinning layers of magic, myth and legend. From the earliest of times, the diamond was revered as a magical intermediary between man and the unseen forces of nature that governed his fate. The stone's awe-inspiring strength and durability came to signify valour and virility, invincibility and good fortune. Its unearthly light symbolised a higher power and spiritual illumination. Through history, this mesmerising mystique has enthralled kings and cardinals, princes and potentates, moguls and movie stars. The diamond evolved into the ultimate possession, with a value that reached way beyond worldly wealth and territorial power.

The word 'diamond' comes from the Greek *adamas* meaning invincible, a term that was used for any particularly hard mineral or material in ancient Greece. But the story of diamonds starts even earlier, some three thousand years ago, in India, where it is thought the earliest diamonds known to man were discovered in the Golconda region of the Deccan, near Hyderabad, in alluvial deposits in the valley between the Godavari and Krishna Rivers. This fabled valley, with its deep, diamond-carpeted pits, was said to be guarded by snakes; miners would send birds to swoop down to pick up the diamonds. The valley is mentioned in Marco Polo's accounts of the wonders of the world, and the second voyage in the fantastical adventures of Sinbad the Sailor revolved around the legend of the diamond-carpeted valley.

The first known reference to diamonds is found in the *Arthashastra* (The Lesson of Profit), a Sanskrit text, probably dating from 320–296 B.C., written by Kautliya, a minister to Chandragupta and founder of the Mauryan Dynasty (322–185 B.C.). It provides information on diamond sources and on the attributes of the diamond, including its ability to scratch a vessel.

From these early times, the diamond was embedded into the very soul of India, its myths and legends woven into the fabric of Hindu culture. Hindus believed that diamonds were created when lightning bolts struck rocks. The Indian deity Krishna gave his love Radha a great diamond – believed by some to be the Koh-i-Noor – to reflect her beauty as it shone in the moonlight, and diamonds were often placed in the eyes of statues. Astrologically, diamonds were associated with sacred moonlight; they were worn in battle as a symbol of courage and virtue, to imbue the wearer with magical strength and also, more practically, to deflect weapon blows. Powdered flawless diamonds were believed to energise and protect, while the powder of flawed diamonds was said to be poisonous. Diamond powder was Catherine de Medici's (1519–1589) poison of choice; she reportedly used it to eliminate certain people who opposed her. A sixth-century A.D. Indian text, the *Ratnapariksha*, describes the protective powers of the diamond in detail, saying that the presence of a diamond means that dangers will recede, and the diamond will protect against serpents, fire, poison, sickness, thieves, floods and evil spirits.

Golconda diamonds possessed unique, unmatched qualities of limpidity, soulful softness and radiant inner light – a light that was preserved by early Indian diamond cutters who polished the stones, subtly, according to their natural crystalline shape. The divine diamonds captivated all who saw them. Indian rulers lusted after them, cheated, tortured and killed for them, exchanged lives for them, and as the diamonds were traded across the known world, mostly by Arab merchants, so they became objects of desire, symbols of power and status, the prerogative and passion of kings and princes.

Legends, myths and beliefs travelled with the diamonds through ancient civilisations, along with an exploration of their extraordinary qualities. By around 500 B.C., coinciding with biblical mentions of the diamond in Aaron's high-priest breastplate and a diamond point for engraving, the Greeks were using diamond splinters for drilling beads and engraving gems for seals. By 168 B.C., the Taoist writer Dongfang Shuo described a diamondiferous floating island.

Opposite: Octahedral diamond crystal discovered in Kimberley, South Africa.

❝❝ Through its history, part of the allure of the divine diamond has always been the challenge of its innate contradictions, the intriguing dualities that endlessly fascinate and captivate, making the diamond ultimately unknowable. One of the rarest substances on earth, the diamond is formed from carbon, one of the most abundant and common elements on the planet. So it is both extraordinary and ordinary. Just as it is science and art, earthly and otherworldly, clarity and mystery, hard and soft, instinct and rationality, material and immaterial – the diamond embodies transformation, metamorphosis, and the journey towards light. Enlightenment. **❞❞**

❝❝ Through De Beers, the diamond came to speak a universal language, conveying its messages of love and luxury. **❞❞**

Opposite: Three De Beers Solitaire Rings: round brilliant, pear shaped, cushion cut. *Following page, left:* One of the world's most legendary diamonds, the Koh-i-Noor is now part of the British Crown Jewels. *Following page, right: Venus transit, second contact,* a photograph by Wolfgang Tillmans, 2004, courtesy of Maureen Paley, London.

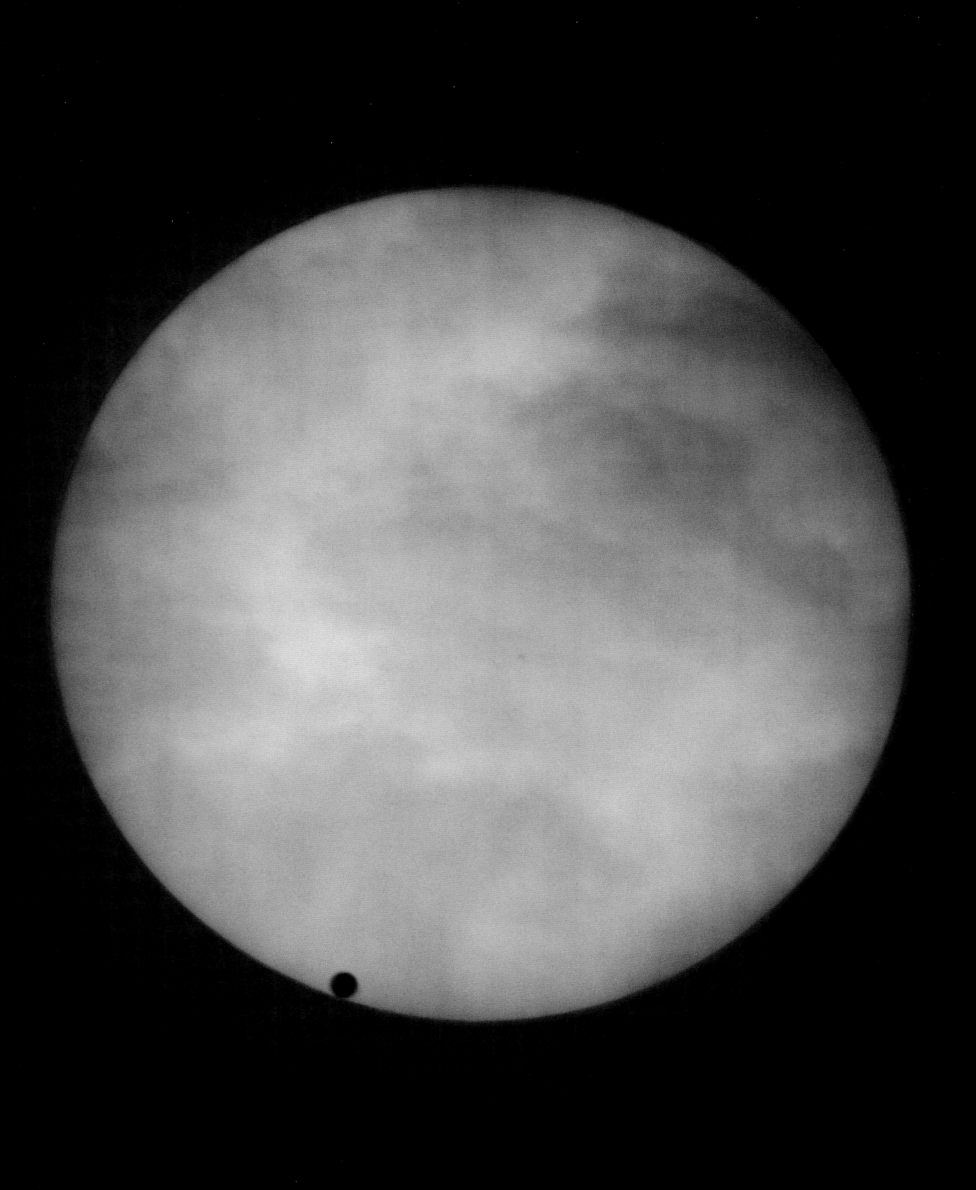

Diamond roughs were first set into jewels around the second century B.C., becoming more widely used in rings in the Roman period, from the second to fourth century A.D., when they were prized for their supernatural powers of bravery and strength, and their ability to triumph over life's tribulations. The ancients engendered their own beliefs: diamonds were slivers of the moon, splinters of falling stars or the tears of the gods. Linking diamonds to everlasting love, Eros' (Cupid's) arrows, unfailingly irresistible, were believed to be tipped with diamonds. Plato worked out that diamonds were the purest, noblest part of gold, condensed into a transparent mass, while he also saw gems as living beings, celestial spirits, which led to later ideas that diamonds were capable of mating and breeding. In the first century A.D., the Roman author and naturalist Pliny the Elder wrote about the physical qualities of the diamond, about the stone's resistance to hammer blows (not strictly true) and fire. He also described Indian stones and their natural crystalline forms. He stated that the diamond was the rarest thing on earth, with a greater value than any other human possession.

In Western Europe, by the early Middle Ages, diamonds were so sought after for their rarity and supposed inherent powers that sumptuary laws decreed they were only to be worn by kings and royalty. Throughout the Middle Ages, the amuletic aspects of minerals and gems and the virtues ascribed to them were more important than their ornamental value, and the many lapidaries – accounts of mystical and medicinal properties of precious stones – strengthened long-held beliefs about the magical effects a diamond could have on the wearer. It was an antidote to poison, could avert bad dreams and strife, impart virtue and generosity, calm the mentally ill and heal the sick if taken into the sickbed to warm the body. A diamond touching each corner of a house or garden offered protection from lightning and storms.

The heyday of the Golconda mines and Indian stones came during the sixteenth and seventeenth centuries, reaching a peak of glory at the height of the mighty Mughal Empire, as the diamond-state came under Mughal rule from 1687. Diamond trading and commerce, centred on the fortress city of Golconda, brought great prosperity and fame to the region, and the name Golconda became a byword for fabulous wealth. Every stone of over two carats automatically belonged to the ruler. The Mughals, both before and after conquering Golconda, amassed magnificent collections. Shah Jahan (ruled 1627–1658), in particular, was an acknowledged gem and diamond connoisseur, whose famed Peacock Throne, sumptuously bejewelled, was set with a massive diamond, often conjectured to have been the Koh-i-Noor.

From the Golconda mines, including the celebrated Kollur Mine, came the world's most historic and fabled diamonds: the Koh-i-Noor, the oldest Golconda diamond, now part of the British Crown Jewels; the Regent, set into Napoleon's coronation sword; the Orlov, given to Catherine the Great; and the infamous, mesmerizing deep-blue diamond, part of the French Crown Jewels and later called the Hope, as celebrated for its alleged curse as for its unrivalled colour and lustre. In Europe at this time, in centres in Germany, France and Bruges in Belgium, under royal patronage and with the encouragement of the French Cardinal Mazarin, himself a diamond devotee, huge progress was being made in diamond cutting. Early cuts evolved into the classic brilliant cut by the end of the seventeenth century, releasing the inner Fire and Brilliance of the stone.

The great French-born merchant-adventurer Jean-Baptiste Tavernier travelled to Asia during six long and adventurous journeys, liaising with the Mughal rulers and bringing back fabulous stones for the diamond-adoring Louis XIV, the Sun King. From India the lust for diamonds rippled out across the world, and while still largely the privilege of royalty and rulers, diamonds were now worn by nobility and aristocracy, by courtiers and courtesans, becoming more common in jewellery after the fourteenth century. Agnès Sorel, the beautiful but low-born favourite mistress of Charles VII of France, is reputed to have been the first commoner to wear diamonds, initiating the age-old and ageless association of diamonds with intense femininity.

Apart from small quantities found in Borneo, from the tenth or even the sixth or seventh century A.D., India remained the world's main source of diamonds until the early eighteenth century when new deposits were discovered in Brazil. The timing was perfect: the Indian

Following page, left: Voynich Manuscript, author unknown, circa early 1400s, courtesy of Beinecke Rare Book and Manuscript Library, Yale University.
Following page, right: Illustration from the De Beers Talisman Collection sketchbook. *Page 22: A Valley of Diamonds and Jewels,* from *The Ascension of Propitious Stars and the Sources of Sovereignty* by al-Su'udi and Sayyid Muhammad ibn Amir Hasan, circa 1582. *Page 23:* The Arabic-inscribed Shah Diamond, a three-centimetre-long yellow diamond with a carat weight of 88.7.

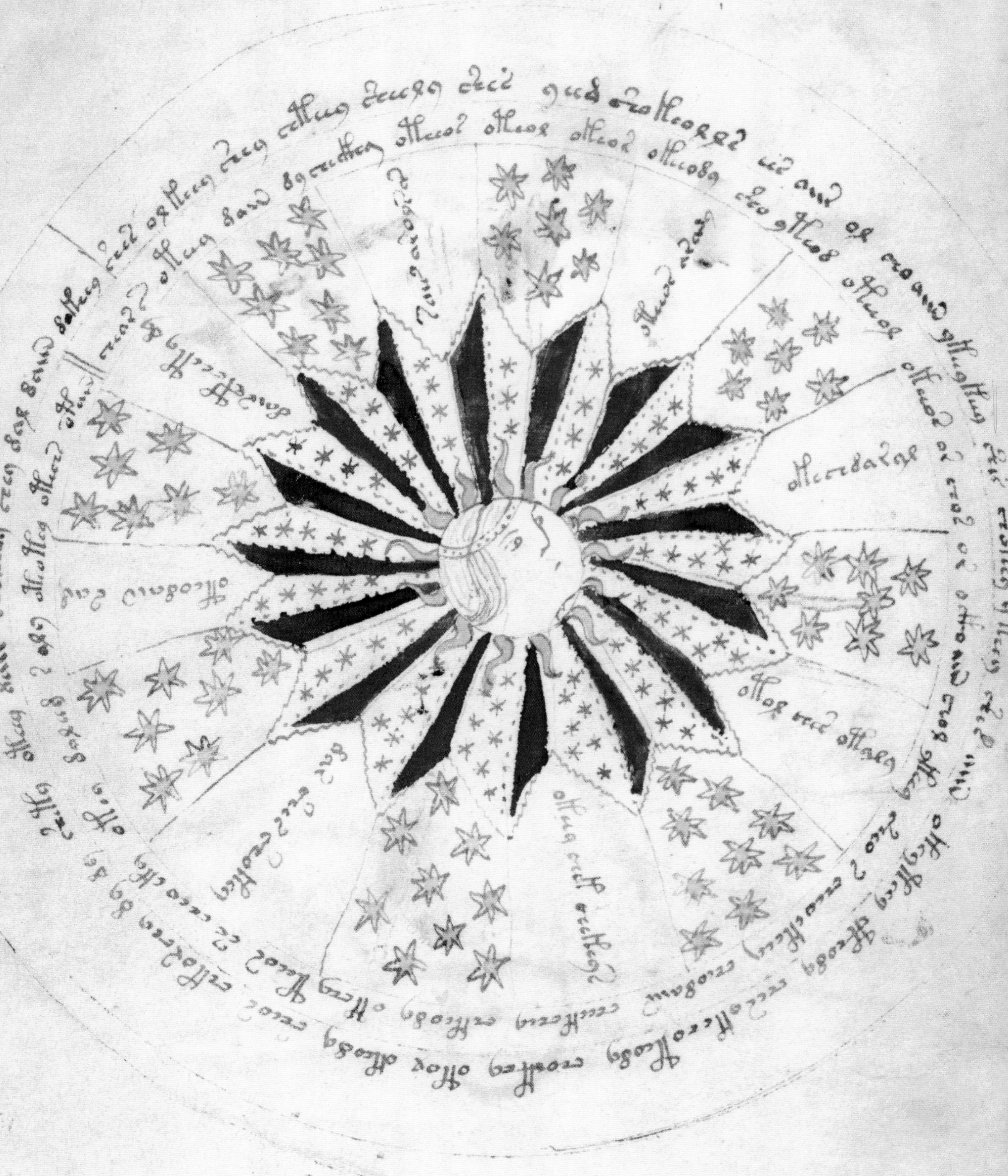

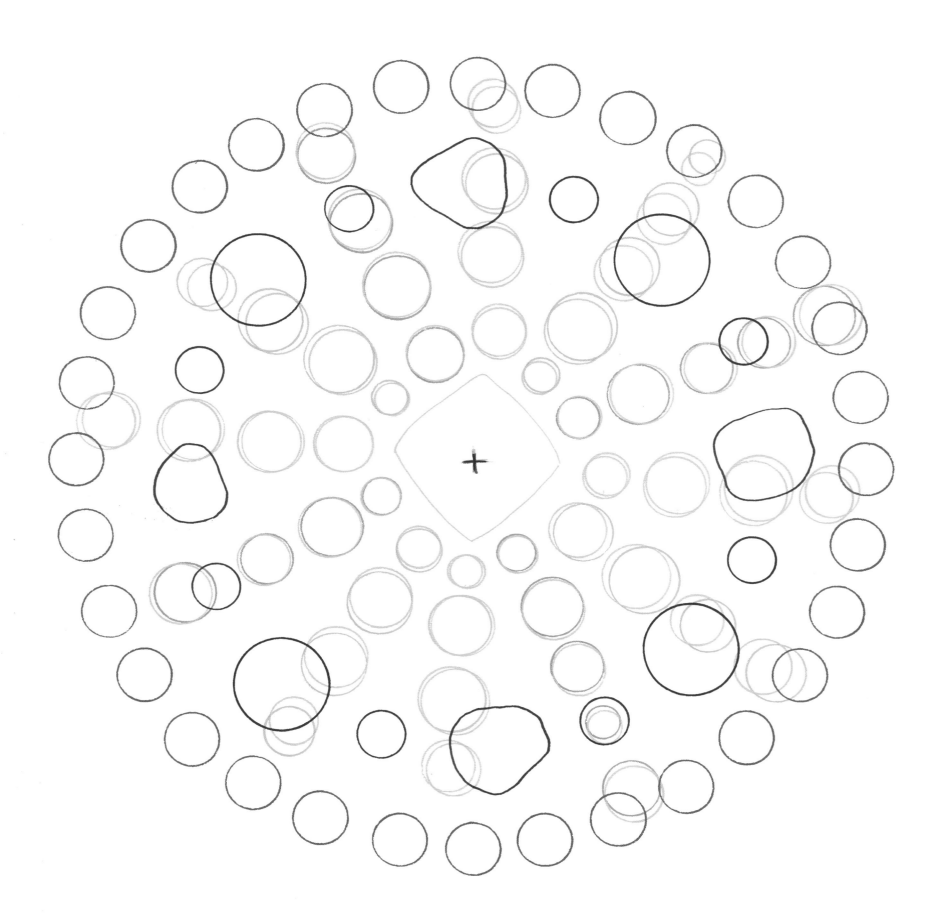

الماس وجواهر وادىسىدر

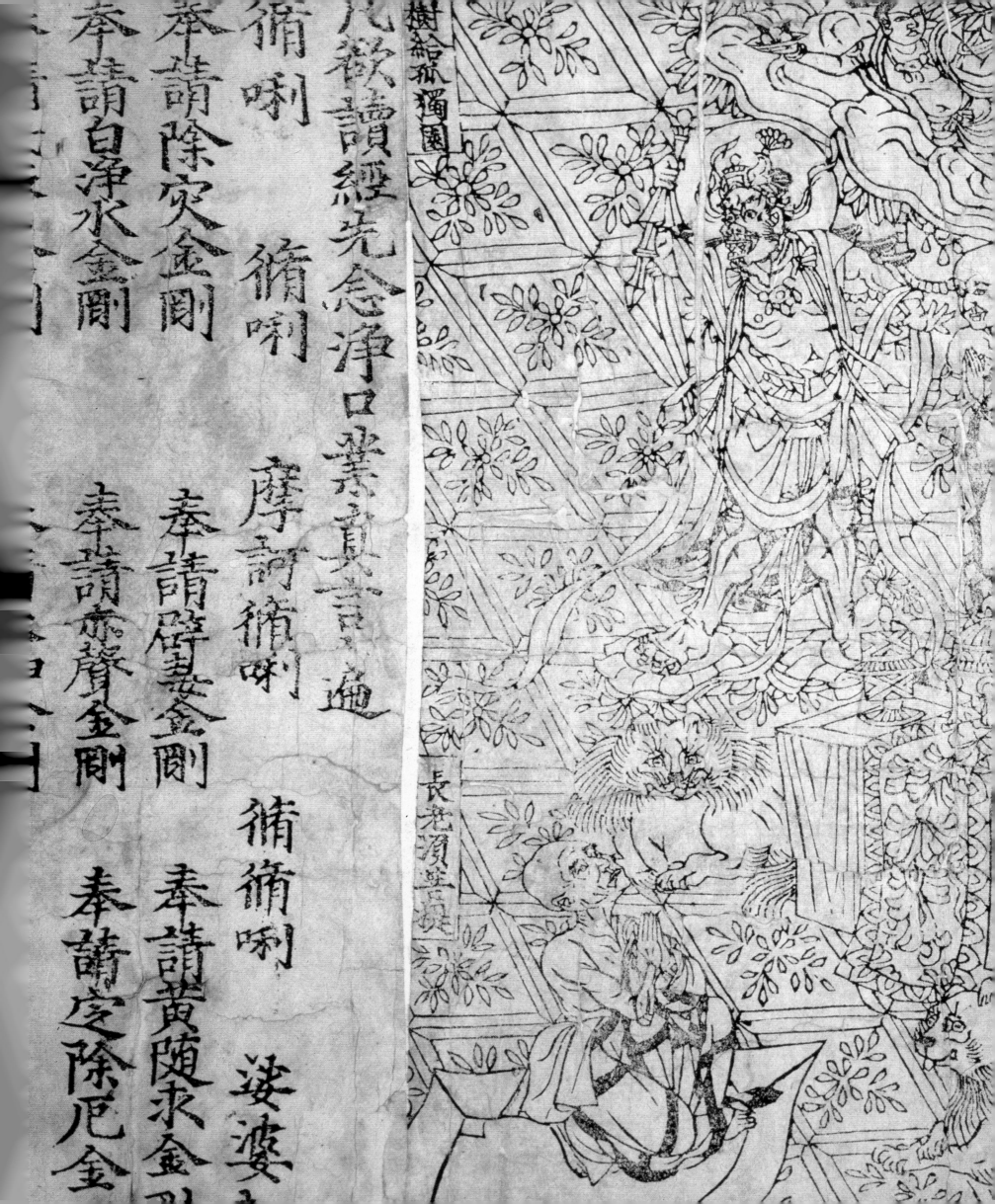

凡欲讀經先念淨口業真言通

循唎　循唎

摩訶循唎

循循唎

婆婆

奉請除突金剛

奉請辟妻金剛

奉請黃隨求金剛

奉請白淨水金剛

奉請赤聲金剛

奉請定除尼金

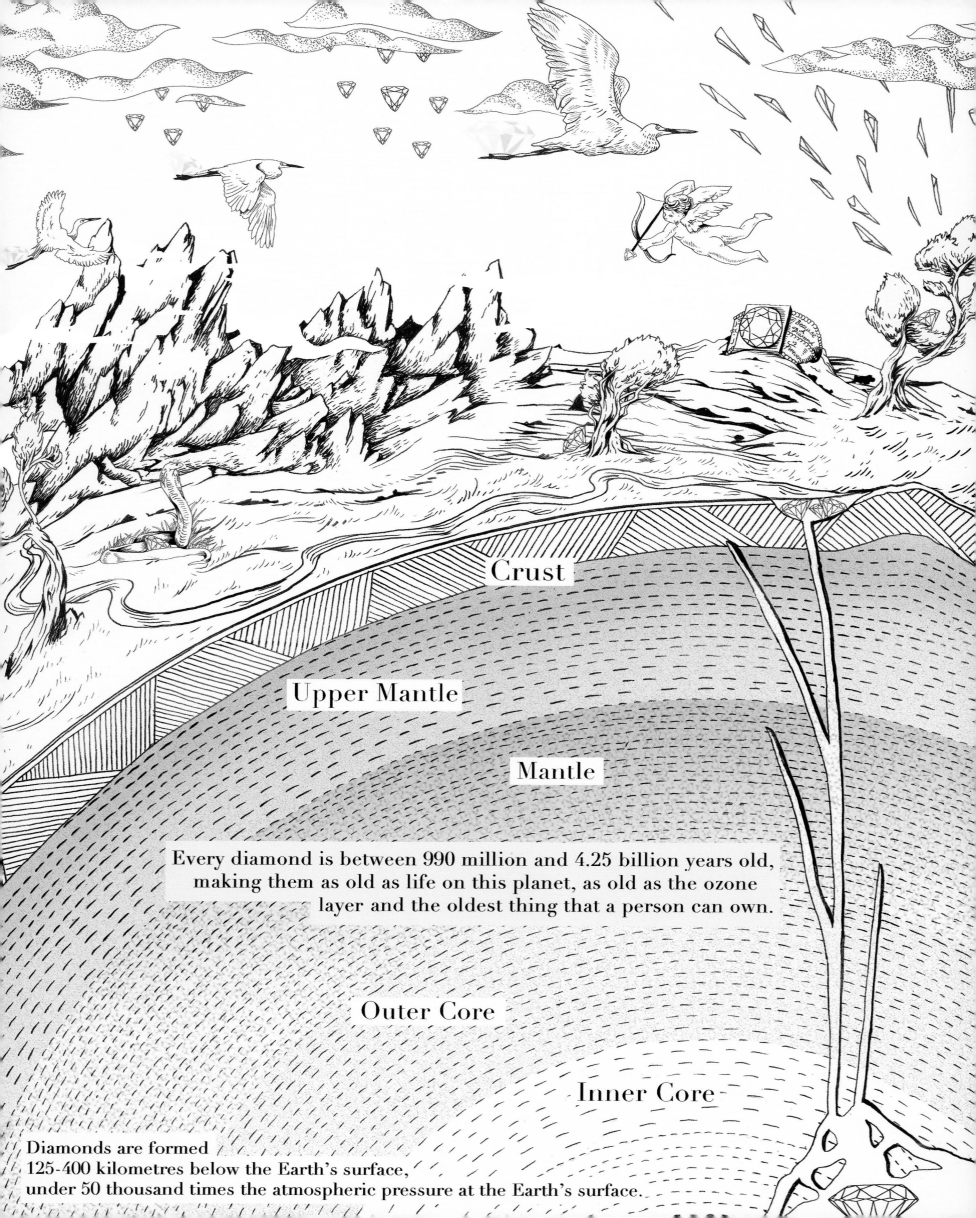

Crust

Upper Mantle

Mantle

Every diamond is between 990 million and 4.25 billion years old, making them as old as life on this planet, as old as the ozone layer and the oldest thing that a person can own.

Outer Core

Inner Core

Diamonds are formed
125-400 kilometres below the Earth's surface,
under 50 thousand times the atmospheric pressure at the Earth's surface.

mines were largely depleted, and the eighteenth century ushered in the age of enlightenment, an age of candlelight, intrigue and glamour. Diamonds became more accessible, more overtly decorative, desperately sought by a new wealthy merchant class eager for the trappings of the aristocracy, the symbols of status and success. Gradually, the ancient and medieval myths and mystical beliefs receded, while the mystique and appeal of the diamond, the lust for its light and luxury, gathered momentum.

The Belle Époque, with its cult of femininity, its newly generated wealth and refined and leisured luxury, set the scene for another great age of the diamond. Newly discovered South African deposits enthralled a clientele of dashing, jewel-bedecked Maharajahs, Oriental potentates, Russian princesses, and most of all fabulously wealthy American tycoons, magnates and industrialists, for whom the diamond was an essential possession, on a par with a country house, carriage and ancestral portraits. This was an era of great diamond transactions, when collectors, with a passion bordering on obsession, avidly pursued the greatest, most historic stones, especially those with royal provenance, like the spectacular Jubilee Diamond, embroidering their fantastic stories with their own tales of luxury, love or tragedy. It was an era too that opened onto a new century, and a new world, in which diamonds, through a process of evolving democratisation, continued to exert their aeons-old fascination as wondrous, mystifying treasures of the earth: indestructible, agelessly modern, rich in romance, filled with unearthly light, loaded with legend linking past, present, future and eternity.

Previous pages: A woodblock print of Buddha preaching to his aged disciple Subhuti from *The Diamond Sutra*, 618–907 A.D. *Opposite: A Diamond is From Forever*, commissioned illustration by Joe Wilson, 2010.

" The Diamond occupies an astoundingly unique place in the story of civilisation. A dazzling fragment of eternity, it has shed its divine light through thousands of years, captivating mankind with its otherworldly beauty. "

" From the earliest of times, the diamond was revered as a magical intermediary between man and the unseen forces of nature that governed his fate. "

Opposite: Emerald-cut three-diamond ring, total weight 7.0 carats. *Following page, left: Clouds II,* a photograph by Wolfgang Tillmans, 2008, courtesy of Maureen Paley, London. *Following page, right: The Triumph of Galatea,* a High Renaissance fresco by Raphael, 1512-14.

MENTOR

De Beers Diamond Jewellers first opened the doors to its flagship store in 2002, onto a new millennium and a new age of the diamond. As concepts of time took on new meaning, all eyes turned to the diamond as a sparkling, celebratory symbol of continuity and eternity, of reassurance and hope for the future. The diamond transcended and defeated time. After the unadorned minimalism of the nineties, sheen, shine and sparkle became the essential ingredients of a 'new millennium style', while the search for purity, meaning and luxury defined the quality of life.

De Beers Diamond Jewellers, established as the quintessential diamond jeweller, tapped into the zeitgeist and gave substance to style, bringing together the diamond's dualities of science and poetry, melding its rich history and long traditions with contemporary creativity and cutting-edge craftsmanship. For a century and more, De Beers diamonds had been set, anonymously, into the creations of master jewellers around the world; now, the finest diamonds, with a peerless pedigree and unparalleled beauty, would have recognition and a home of their own at De Beers Diamond Jewellers. With a name that resonates across the globe, synonymous with diamonds, but also with quality and perfection, adventure and exploration, De Beers Diamond Jewellers has a dual heritage: founded on the unrivalled expertise and experience of the De Beers family of companies; and backed by the style, design excellence and affinity with the luxury of the mighty LVMH (Moët Hennessy Louis Vuitton) group.

Just as the diamond mines in Brazil were becoming depleted in the mid nineteenth century, huge new deposits were discovered in South Africa. The story, well documented, shaped the course of South Africa's history: It begins in 1866, when a poor farmer's son, fifteen-year-old Erasmus Jacobs, picked up a 'pretty stone' on the banks of the Orange River in Cape Colony. A curiosity, it was passed around and eventually identified as a diamond. Weighing approximately twenty-one carats, with a pale yellow hue, the stone was named the Eureka; one hundred years later, the Eureka was purchased by De Beers and presented to the people of South Africa. In Europe, however, the stone was greeted with little enthusiasm and a great deal of sceptical derision. The idea of diamonds in South Africa seemed ridiculously

Opposite: Ghost, Olive No. 13,
a photograph of Galilee by Ori
Gersht, 2004.

far-fetched. Until, that is, in 1869, when a Griqua shepherd found another diamond, this time of 83.5 carats, which was sold for five hundred sheep, ten head of cattle and a horse – a fortune to the shepherd. The stone, named the Star of South Africa, sparked a great diamond rush, drawing diggers and fortune hunters from around the world to the banks of the Orange and Vaal Rivers. Before long, major deposits, known as 'dry diggings', which were actually kimberlite pipes, were discovered further inland. The two most significant mines were on a farm owned by two brothers, Johannes Nicolaas and Diederik Arnoldus De Beer. The mines were later known as the De Beers and Kimberley, after the British Secretary of State for the Colonies, Lord Kimberley. Eventually the De Beer brothers sold their farm and moved on. In 1873, a young Englishman, Cecil John Rhodes, was sent to South Africa for his health. Rhodes began by selling water and then pumps to prospectors, and soon bought his first claim in the De Beers Mine. He understood the huge potential of diamonds for the country but also saw the need to regulate the chaotic throng of competing miners through a system of consolidation and a single sales channel. He acquired more and more stakes, and in 1880 founded the De Beers Mining Company, becoming Prime Minister of Cape Colony in 1890. His main competition came from Barney Barnato, owner of the Kimberley Mine, and in 1888, after a protracted battle for supremacy, they joined forces to form De Beers Consolidated Mines Ltd. In 1890, at Rhodes' invitation, the London Diamond Syndicate was formed.

The new mines were to produce some of the world's most spectacular and historic stones, starting with the Jubilee Diamond, discovered at Jagersfontein Mine in 1895 and weighing in at 650.80 carats. But in 1905, the world's largest rough diamond, a monumental 3,106 carats, was discovered at the Premier Mine, later renamed the Cullinan Mine, becoming part of De Beers Consolidated Mines in 1917. The stone was presented to King Edward VII for his sixty-sixth birthday and was later cut and polished into nine important diamonds. The largest two, the Cullinan I (530.2 carats) and the Cullinan II (317.4 carats) now form part of the British Crown Jewels.

Rhodes' pre-eminent position in the diamond industry was taken over by Ernest Oppenheimer. German-born, he had worked for diamond brokers in London, and, at the age of twenty-two, was sent by them to Kimberley as a buyer, arriving there in 1902, the year Rhodes died. Oppenheimer rose to become Mayor of Kimberley in 1912, and in 1917 founded the Anglo American Corporation, which was to be the world's largest mining group. He took over German diamond interests in South West Africa (now Namibia), creating Consolidated Diamond Mines of South West Africa, which he offered to De Beers in return for stock, taking a seat on the board in 1926 and becoming chairman in 1929.

Oppenheimer perpetuated Rhodes' vision and strengthened his single-channel marketing strategy, co-ordinating and regulating the worldwide supply of diamonds through a producers' co-operative. Throughout the twentieth century, new deposits were discovered in Africa, as well as in Russia, Australia and Canada, and the De Beers Group remained at the forefront of the industry, conscientious custodians of value and quality, bringing stability to the market. They also led the way in promoting diamonds, telling their story, shaping their image for each decade and each new generation: throughout the golden years of Hollywood; the fifties with its sophistication, femininity and Marilyn Monroe; the jet-set glamour of the sixties and seventies; the post-feminist glitz of the eighties; and the minimalism of the nineties. Through De Beers, the diamond came to speak a universal language, conveying its messages of love and luxury, even in cultures and countries with no previous associations or attachment to the stone or even to Western concepts of jewellery wearing, such as Japan.

In 1939, De Beers initiated a trailblazing marketing strategy on behalf of the entire diamond industry, aimed at demystifying the diamond yet building its mystique, revealing its full allure and underlining its meaning – in short, romancing the stone. The company approached a leading U.S. advertising agency, N.W. Ayer based in New York, to run an advertising campaign nationwide that year, to stimulate interest and conquer the vast American market. Then, in 1947, Frances Gerety, a young N.W. Ayer copywriter assigned to the De Beers account, was given the brief to come up with a line to encompass and express both the physical attributes of the diamond and its romance. Legend has it that she was working late one night, wrestling with the brief and its seemingly impossible challenge. About to give up for the night, she put her head down on the desk, thinking, 'Please God, send me a line',

Cheque for £5,338,650 paid to Kimberley Central by De Beers to assume complete control over the Kimberley Mine on 18 July 1889.

Kimberley Mine, 1902. Loading tailings with a steam shovel (the tailings have collapsed, engulfing the machine).

Drawing of the farm owned by the De Beers brothers where the first diamonds were found in South Africa in the 1800s.

The 601-carat Lesotho Diamond, found on 26 May 1967 by Mrs. Ernestinea Ramaboa. Later cut into 18 gems.

The cleaving of the Cullinan Diamond, the largest rough diamond ever recorded, discovered in 1905.

Tools used for the cutting of the 3,106-carat Cullinan Diamond.

De Beers Group Diamond Sorter, 1950s.

Erasmus Stephanus Jacobs, the discoverer of the Eureka Diamond – the first diamond found in South Africa. Jacobs made the discovery in 1866, at the age of 15.

The Williamson Pink Diamond in the rough.
weighing 54 carats.

The Williamson Pink Diamond as it was presented to H.R.H The Princess Elizabeth.
on the occasion of her marriage. by Dr. J.T. Williamson.

    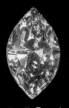 

1. 85 cts.   2.87 cts.   5.70 cts.   6.4 4 cts.   11.35 cts.   27.34 cts.

22.27 cts.   53.96 cts.   30.15 cts.   23.01 cts.   143.20 cts.

The Star of Sierra Leone yielded 17 gems. of which 11 are shown here.
The rough diamond, found in 1972. weighed 968.9 carats.

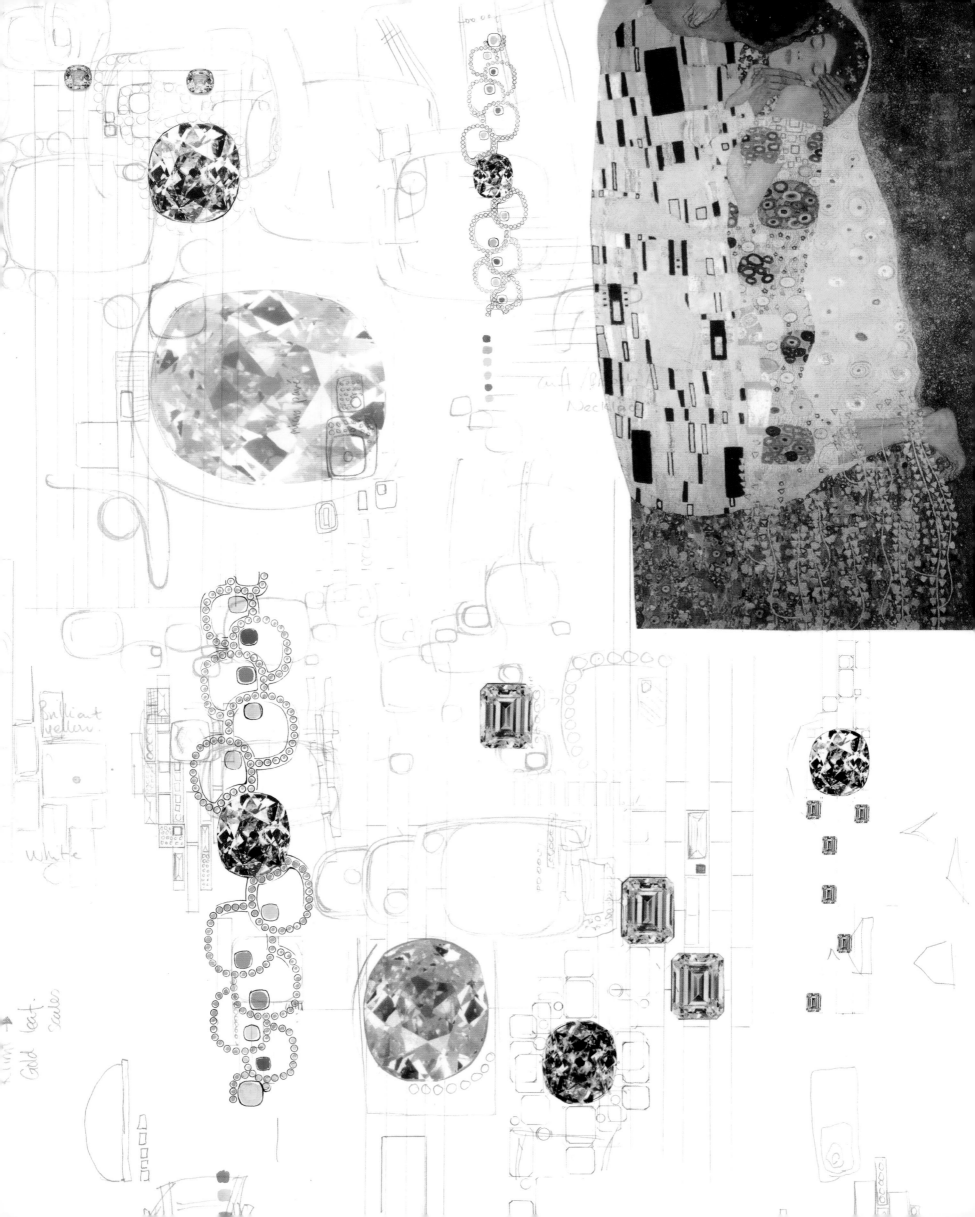

and then scribbled 'A Diamond is Forever'. It was a stroke of genius: the indestructibility of the diamond, its eternity, linked, simply, to everlasting love. The catchphrase – equally powerful translated into languages around the globe – was to achieve worldwide fame and success, so much so that fifty years later it was voted the top advertising slogan of the twentieth century.

Advertisements in the fifties expanded on the phrase, saying, 'May your happiness last as long as your diamond', accompanied by paintings commissioned from famous contemporary artists – bringing modernity and relevance – and a poem, positioning the diamond engagement ring as the quintessential symbol of undying love and commitment. From here, the diamond became an integral part of the whole modern-day ritual and ceremony of love, engagement and marriage. In 1956, Ian Fleming used the phrase for the title of one of his series of James Bond novels, made into a movie with Sean Connery in 1971, guaranteeing the diamond and its associations with foreverness a place in modern-day culture.

At the same time, De Beers realised the importance of design and creativity in keeping the diamond jewellery industry dynamic, engaging and relevant to its moment in time. In 1953 they launched a biannual international design competition, the Diamonds International Awards, which continued until 2000, leading diamonds along a path of intense glamour and cutting-edge design, both nurturing emerging talent around the world and linking diamonds to the biggest names in the international creative community. The Diamonds International Awards, heralded in its day as the haute couture of the jewellery world, became a high-profile, hotly anticipated event, celebrating innovation, ingenuity and design excellence.

In step with a fast-changing world, since the end of the last century the De Beers family of companies has changed its structure and strategy, shifting the emphasis away from its measured control of the diamond supply line onto the diamond itself – its identity, quality, rarity and personality – and onto the dreams and desires of the discerning jewellery client. Today, the company controls about forty percent of the world diamond trade. As part of

Previous page, left: The De Beers Centenary Diamond, with a weight of 273.85 carats, is the third-largest diamond ever to have been produced by the Premier Mine. The diamond is colour-graded 'D' by the GIA, the highest grade of colourless diamond. It is both internally and externally flawless. *Previous page, right:* Illustrations using the Centenary Diamond from the De Beers sketchbook. *Opposite:* Illustrations using famous diamonds from the De Beers sketchbook, including the Eureka Diamond and the Kimberley Diamond, discovered in 1921. Collaged element from Gustav Klimt's *The Kiss*, 1907-1908.

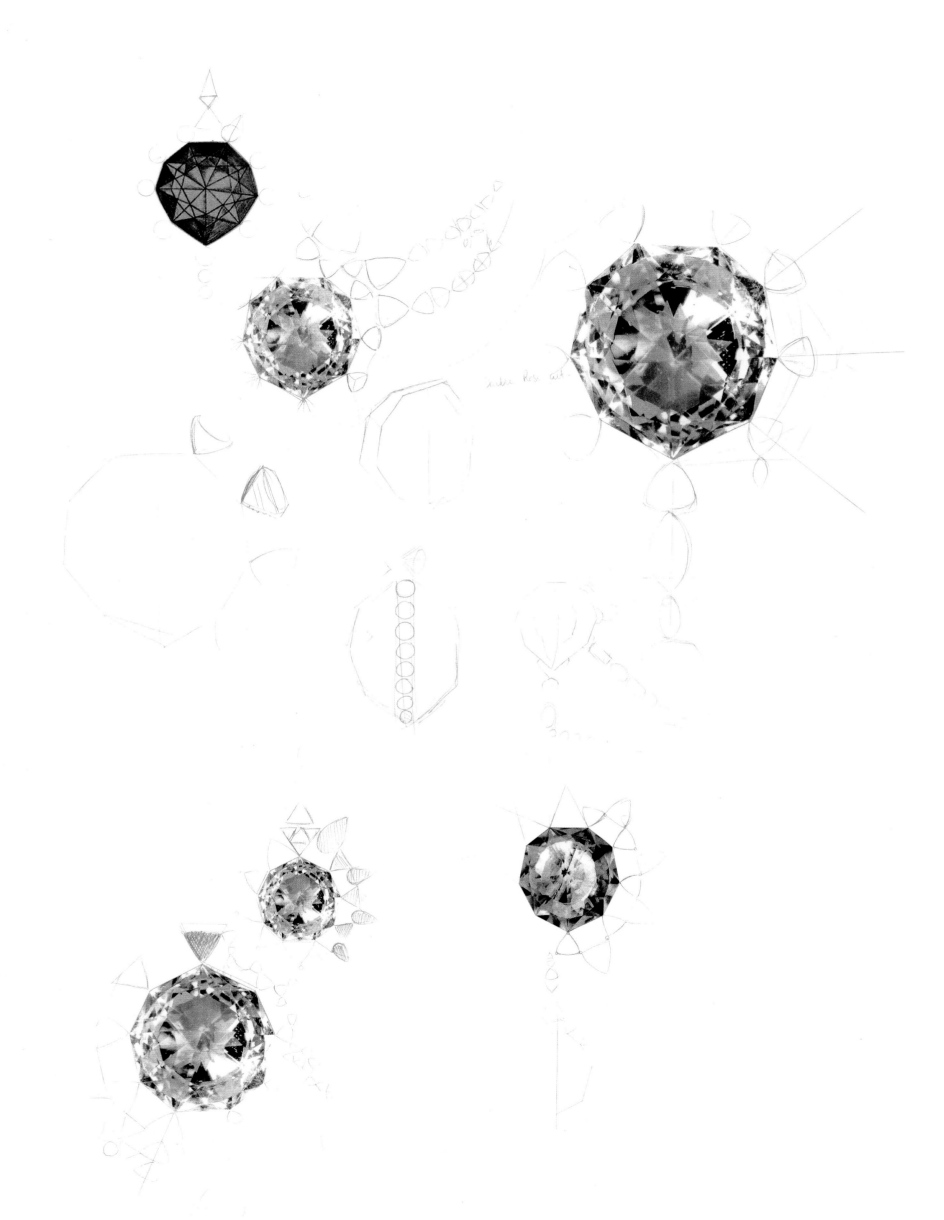

their ongoing commitment to corporate responsibility, they have focused on improving health, education and living standards in the countries in which they operate. With growing concerns over conflict diamonds, De Beers took the decision to handle only diamonds of certain origin, guaranteeing total integrity, truth and transparency throughout the supply chain, from the mine to the retailer. In a newly balanced relationship, the client has become part of the creative process, from the selection of the stone itself to the design of the finished jewel.

As part of this evolution, the De Beers Group realised the huge potential for a diamond brand that not only bore their name but also carried their values, their dedication to perfection and their passion for the diamond to an increasingly discerning and educated clientele.

The creation of De Beers Diamond Jewellers in 2001 has played a vital role in this new empowerment and involvement of the client, encapsulating the De Beers legend and adventure, and distilling its unrivalled expertise and experience into dynamically designed contemporary jewellery, so that creativity and modernity are underpinned with tradition and trust. In this way, De Beers has made a major contribution to the recent democratisation of the diamond. The past few decades have seen one of the most significant turns in the story of the diamond, possibly since the eighteenth century, as taboos are broken, conventions crushed and rules overturned. The diamond, once representing a social divide, has become socially inclusive, accessible, desirable to all generations and ages, worn for day or night, formal or casual, classic or sporty, the most powerful expression of individual style.

Previous page, left: The Florentine Diamond, a nine-sided, 126-facet double-rose cut of yellow colour, with a weight of 137.27 carats. *Previous page, right:* Sketches of the jewellery designs created for the Florentine Diamond. *Opposite:* Sketches of jewellery designs created for the Florentine Diamond with full yellow colour.

"A Diamond is Forever."

"The creation of De Beers Diamond Jewellers in 2001 has played a vital role in this new empowerment and involvement of the client, encapsulating the De Beers legend and adventure, and distilling its unrivalled expertise and experience into dynamically designed contemporary jewellery, so that creativity and modernity are underpinned with tradition and trust."

Opposite: A De Beers Aura Ring, cushion cut, on an original De Beers Group historical advertisement. *Following pages:* Vintage advertisements from the De Beers Group Archives, courtesy of the De Beers Group. *Page 52: The Miracle of Love,* vintage advertisement featuring *Message of Love,* painted for the De Beers Collection by Pierre Ino, 1956. *Page 53: Lovely Miracle... Just For You,* vintage advertisement featuring *Lovely Miracle,* painted for the De Beers Collection by Robert Grilley, 1958.

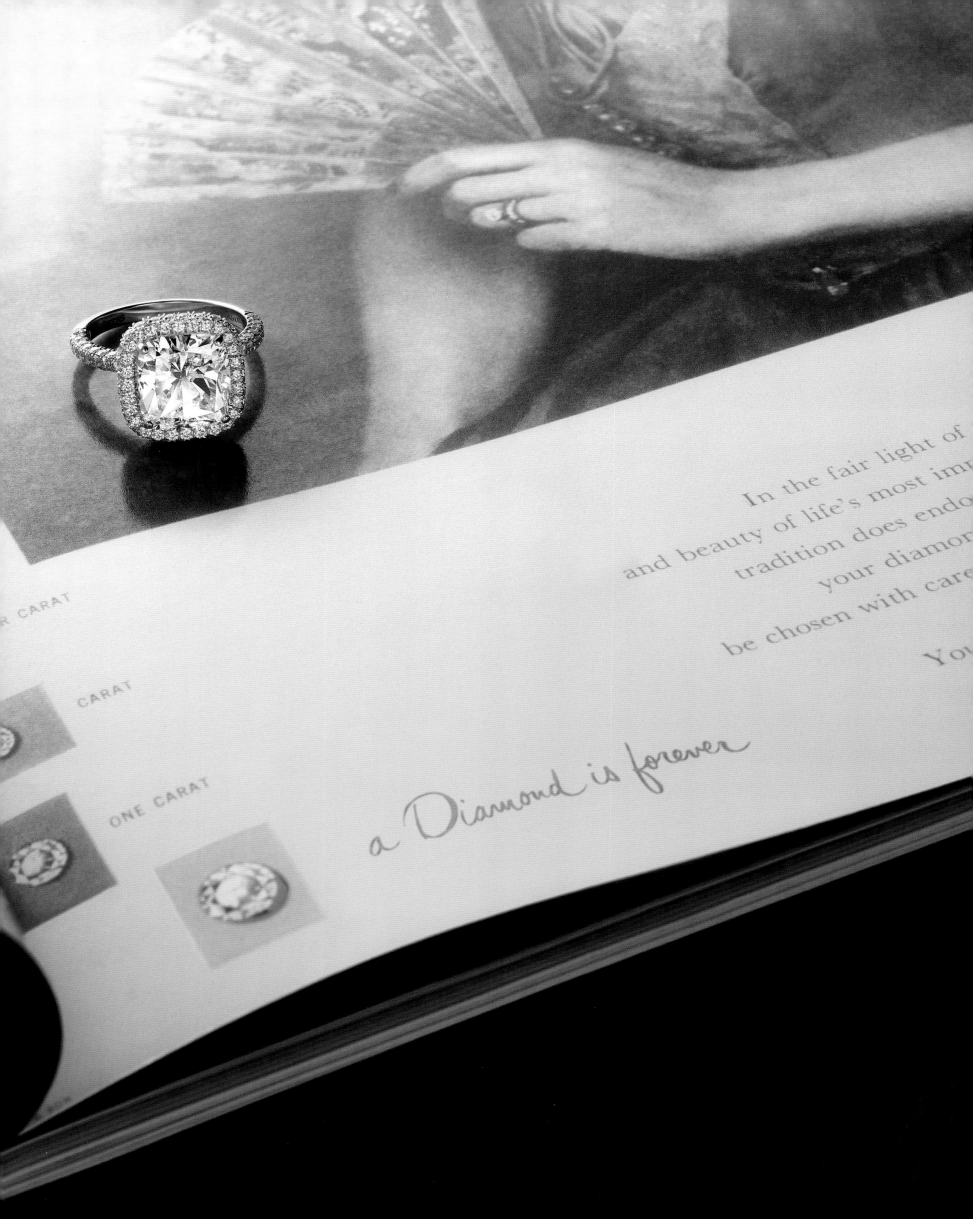

In the fair light of
and beauty of life's most imp
tradition does endu
your diamon
be chosen with care

You

a Diamond is forever

CARAT

ONE CARAT

A DIAMOND IS FOREVER

How far its beam A little light, so constant and so ...
it finds his heart across the widest waters and hou...
That is his diamond on her finger — an ever-fixéd ...
to safe home-comings and fair rewards in their new ...

Joan
Thank you, darling,
for making us a
family! Tom

De Beers Consolidated Mines, Ltd.

A DIAMOND IS FOREVER

A diamond gift that shines so jubilantly to mark a great moment . . . the
anniversary, an important birthday, a daughter's debut,
ingful event . . . will recall the occasion always. A trusted
course, be consulted.

determined by color, cutting, and clarity, as well as carat weight. A two-carat diamond, for
$3350, plus tax, at representative jewelers. Exceptionally fine stones are higher priced.

Lovely miracle . . . just for you

A DIAMOND IS FOREVER

To mark a great occasion

. . . how appropriate it is that a man may express the thoughts that stir
his heart in the steadfast radiance of a diamond. The diamond gift that
marks a great occasion . . . an anniversary, an important birthday, the
birth of a child, a daughter's debut, or a specially meaningful event . . . will
recall the moment always. A trusted jeweler should, of course, be consulted.

The value of a diamond is determined by color, cutting and clarity, as well as carat weight. A two-carat diamond, for
instance, ranges from $1260 to $3350, plus tax, at representative jewelers. Exceptionally fine stones are higher priced.

A diamond is forever

De Beers Consolidated Mines, Ltd.

o light a lover's dream

en love is new and fancy spins its myriad enchant-
nts, an engagement diamond shines in gay accord. For
girl who wears it, and the man who shares her married
d, it will recall their first happiness, always . . . and
of their love in brilliant beauty until the end of time.

diamond is forever

Message of Love—painted for the De Beers Collection by Pierre Ino

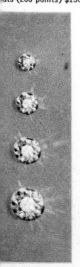
The miracle of love

A girl's joy, flowering like a rose, is radiant and full in the
lovely miracle of love awakening. And for her a star,
blazing bright as her dreams, will recall this moment always.
Her engagement diamond, fair spark of eternity,
reflects the light of her happiness in changeless splendor,
and treasures its tender message of love until the end of time.

Remember, color, cutting and clarity,
as well as carat weight, contribute to
a diamond's beauty and value.
A trusted jeweler is your best adviser.
Extended payments can usually be arranged.

Lovely miracle . . . painted for the De Beers Collection by Robert Grilley.

De Beers Consolidated Mines, Ltd.

Lovely miracle... *just for you*

In the springtime of love, the flowers smile more sweetly, lend their magic to your dreams. And, from earth, too, your engagement diamond joins them, a lovely miracle to tell your new-found joys. Lit for eternity, this fairest talisman will recount your love's continuing story . . . the hopes fulfilled, the strivings and rewards of later years . . . for you and for your children's children, until time's end.

A DIAMOND IS FOREVER

INTEGRITY

The relationship between jeweller and client is a very personal one, involving trust, confidence and sensitivity. Traditionally, in India a jeweller or goldsmith – who would often live at court – was considered as important, and as personal, as a physician or astrologer. Today, that relationship based on mutual trust and understanding remains crucial to the experience of buying a diamond jewel – a process in which emotion and intuition must be balanced with a rational assessment of the quality and integrity of both the diamond itself and the skilled craftsmanship that shapes the jewel. De Beers is, and has always been, the world's leading diamond mentor, with unmatched credentials and more than a century of experience. From the beginning, De Beers Diamond Jewellers set out to bring this legacy of grassroots authority and insider knowledge into the realm of contemporary jewellery and ultimately to the customer, to use its expertise to raise the bar and exceed expectations. The aim was to demystify the process of choosing a diamond without diminishing its innate mystique, and at the same time to set new standards of integrity and excellence for the world of precious jewellery.

The diamond selection process at De Beers Diamond Jewellers is considered the most rigorous possible in the jewellery world today; each single diamond bought on the open market is closely examined, evaluated and hand-chosen by a highly experienced expert, to meet acutely exacting criteria as set out by the De Beers Institute of Diamonds. This body of experts, a team of the most revered diamond authorities in the world and unique to De Beers Diamond Jewellers, oversees all diamond selection and buying on the open market and scrupulously monitors quality, sustainability and ethical practices throughout the supply chain. They also established the brand's unique insistence on the brilliance of all diamonds used by De Beers Diamond Jewellers – brilliance that depends on the perfection of the cut and polish, as well as the intrinsic qualities of the rough diamond as dictated by Mother Nature. The Institute was responsible for developing a new standard for evaluating

Previous page, left: The Rose Gardens (display) (IV) by Sarah Jones, c-type print mounted on aluminium, 2009, courtesy of Maureen Paley, London. *Previous page, right:* Adonis Rose Solitaire Ring from the De Beers Adonis Rose Collection. Designed platinum band with bezel-set marquise diamonds, pavé round brilliant diamonds and a claw-set centre diamond. Adonis Rose Band from the De Beers Adonis Rose Collection. Designed white gold band with bezel-set marquise diamonds and pavé round brilliant diamonds.

diamonds, looking, above all, for Fire, Life and Brilliance.

First and foremost, all De Beers diamonds must be entirely natural and untreated, and all diamonds must be ethically sourced, conforming to not only the Kimberley Process but to the more stringent De Beers Group's Best Practice Principles that ensure no child labour has been involved at any stage. The Kimberley Process, ratified in 2002 and implemented in 2003, is a system, with a United Nations mandate, supported by governments, the global diamond industry and non-governmental organisations, designed to prevent diamonds from areas of conflict from entering the legitimate supply chain. This in turn prevents rough diamonds from being used by rebel groups to fund conflict. Through the Kimberley Process, rough diamonds are monitored at every point in the supply chain from mine to retail, ensuring, among other precautions, that shipments are transported in secure containers with government-validated certificates, so that no uncertified shipments of rough diamonds are allowed to leave or enter a country participating

Opposite: Artist's rendering of the De Beers philosophy behind selecting the world's most beautiful diamonds. *Following pages:* Diamond sorters carefully sifting through rough diamonds in search of the most beautiful specimens. Image courtesy of the De Beers Group Archives.

DE BEERS
JEWELLERY

make it more beautiful

34.5°

*○

'Firist', max 1.20

41.0°
Each facet
must be within
0.70°

Table 58% max, with depth
60.9% minimum.
* remove outside
check for arrowhead reflection
in bezel facets.

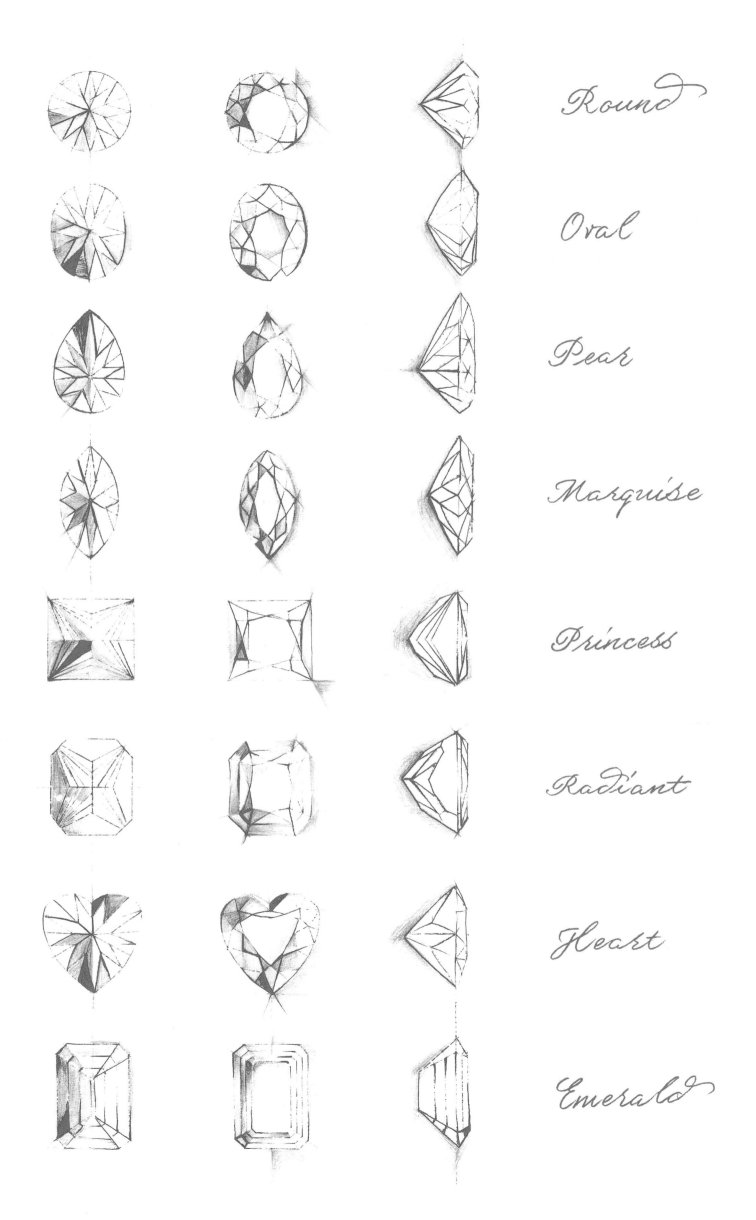

Round

Oval

Pear

Marquise

Princess

Radiant

Heart

Emerald

in the process. To date, seventy-four countries have joined the Kimberley Process, and while ninety-nine percent of all diamonds are certified through the Process to be free from conflict, one hundred percent of De Beers Diamond Jewellers' diamonds are guaranteed to be conflict free.

The Kimberley Process is backed up by a chain of warranties covering all buyers and sellers of both rough and polished diamonds. De Beers Diamond Jewellers deals only with suppliers of impeccable reputation and integrity. Once the ethics, legitimacy and authenticity of the diamonds are assured, only then does one of De Beers Diamond Jewellers' leading experts begin the process of evaluation, checking every diamond over 0.2 carat. Out of twenty to thirty thousand diamonds examined over a year's period, only twelve to fifteen thousand will be selected. Smaller hand-selected stones for pavé work, under 0.2 carats, are also subject to the same standards of quality. The De Beers Diamond Jewellers expert first examines the diamond for colour, comparing each stone to a De Beers Ideal Master Diamond in order to make an assessment; then for clarity, following industry standards that are further qualified by the individual expert's long diamond-grading experience. Then, looking beyond the accepted standards of diamond grading, the cut is evaluated in minute detail – the proportions, the symmetry and the critical angles – to assess the level of Fire, Life and Brilliance. A De Beers expert's eye can see immediately if a diamond meets the company's exacting standards of perfection, sparkle and beauty. This extra crucial step in the selection process means that every diamond in every De Beers Diamond Jewellers creation is not only of superlative quality but also of exceptional brilliance, ensuring an unrivalled consistency of quality and lustre in all De Beers jewellery. In pursuit of perfection, De Beers' in-house diamond experts will often travel to suppliers to work closely with cutters and polishers to help them achieve De Beers Diamond Jewellers' exceptional standards of brilliance.

The added dimension of dedication to brilliance in the brand's own process of evaluation, their scrupulous insistence on perfect cut and proportions, and their skill in unleashing the full beauty and light are what sets De Beers Diamond Jewellers apart.

Page 62: The Incomparable III, a painting of a De Beers diamond by Damien Hirst, 2008, courtesy of Hirst Holdings Limited and Damien Hirst. *Page 63:* Vintage illustration of the classic diamond shapes and cuts. *Previous page, left:* Run off of rough diamonds from a De Beers Mine in South Africa, courtesy of the De Beers Group Archives. *Previous page, right:* Detail of etched glass from a De Beers Diamond Jewellers store concept. *Opposite:* Andrew Coxon, founder of the De Beers Diamond Institute.

Diamonds are generally classified by the criteria set out in the '4 Cs' – cut, carat, colour and clarity – standards of evaluation that had been developed with the Gemological Institute of America (GIA) but were then simplified and formulated into the easily understandable '4 Cs' concept by De Beers themselves and introduced to the public in 1939.

'Carat' refers to the weight of a diamond. Each carat is divided into one hundred points and is equivalent to 0.2 grams, a measurement adopted in the United States in 1913 and now universal. The name comes from the carob seed, used by early traders as near-uniform counterweights to balance their scales.

In terms of colour, the finest white diamonds (as opposed to fancy coloured diamonds) should be as close to colourless as possible. Colour grading as defined by the GIA is classified by letters of the alphabet, the best being D, colourless, and continuing through G to J, near colourless, right down to Z. Colour gradations for each letter are subtle but clearly defined to the professional eye. The letter D was chosen to represent the top white diamond colour, as other pre-existing, imprecise and confusing classifications had used letters A, B and C among other labels.

Clarity indicates the presence (or lack) of inclusions inside the stone, as well as external marks or blemishes. Most diamonds contain minute inner flaws or inclusions, often referred to as 'birthmarks', as they occurred during the long formation process of the diamond, over millions or billions of years under extreme heat and pressure deep within the earth's core. Clarity is graded according to the visibility of inclusions or blemishes under tenfold magnification. The top grade, reserved for the rarest and most highly prized diamonds, is flawless (FL), showing no inclusions or blemishes. This ranges downwards through IF, internally flawless, meaning only blemishes and no inclusions; VVSI, meaning very, very slight inclusions, difficult to see under magnification even for an experienced grader; VS, very slight; SI, slight; down to I, obvious inclusions which ultimately affect sparkle.

Opposite: Artist's interpretation of the De Beers Iris, collage on paper, 2010. *Previous page, left:* Printed scan from the De Beers Iris. *Previous page, right:* Photograph of the Louvre's glass and metal pyramid, designed by I. M. Pei, courtesy of the Louvre, Paris.

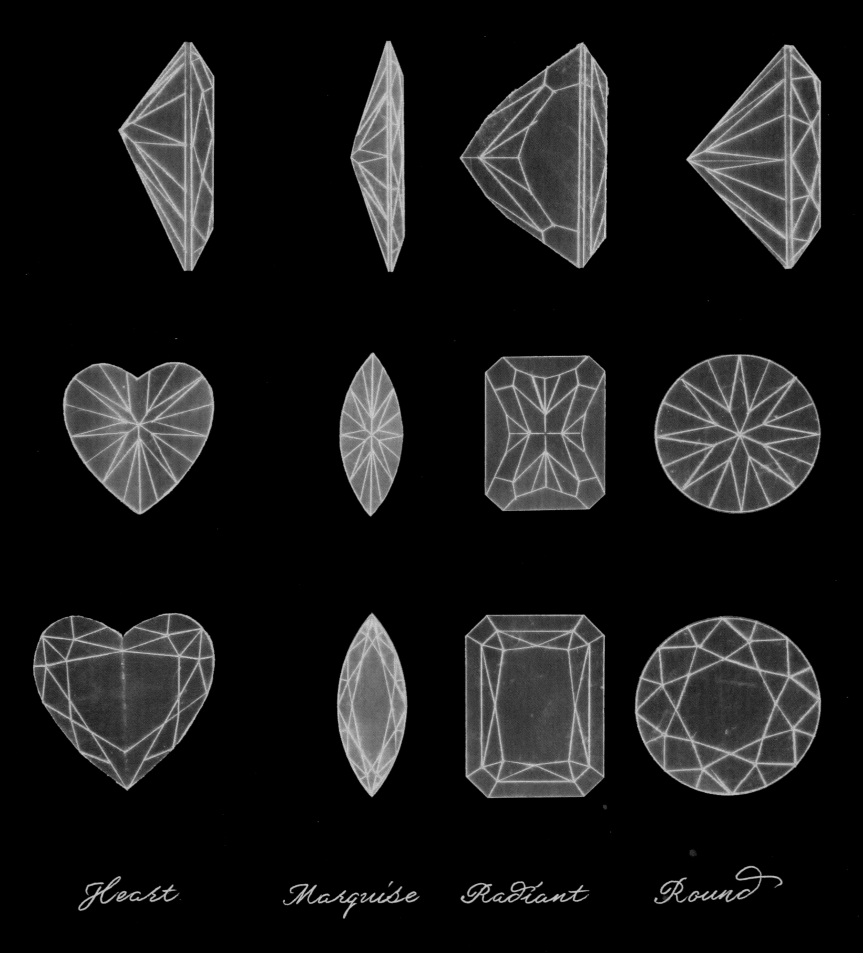

Heart   Marquise   Radiant   Round

Pear   *Oval*   *Princess*   *Emerald*

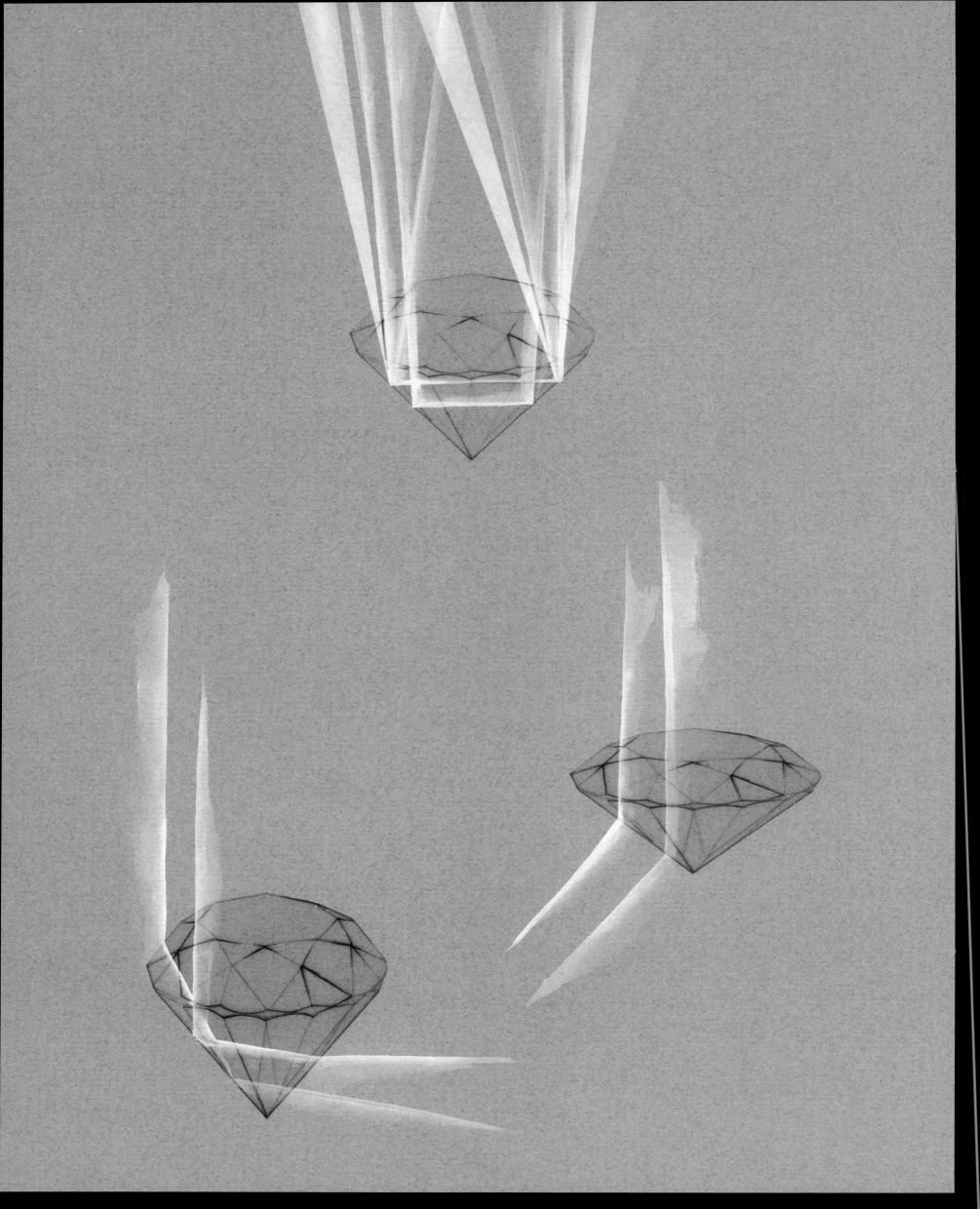

Cut is the most crucial of the 4 Cs, especially at De Beers Diamond Jewellers, as it not only governs shape but affects and influences the Fire, Life and Brilliance of a diamond. Brilliance refers to the overall natural transparency and brightness of the diamond; Fire is the dispersion of light into the rainbow colours of the spectrum; and Life is the movement of light within a stone, or scintillation. Aside from the shape of the stone, from the classic round brilliant to fancy cuts, a cut is evaluated on the precision of its critical angles, its symmetry, proportions and polish. Proportions concern the relationships between the different parts of the diamond: the table (top flat facet), the crown (visible top of the stone), the girdle (the line or edge around the middle of the stone) and the pavilion (the underside). These relationships can affect the way the stone interacts with light.

While the 4 Cs remain the standard criteria within the jewellery world today, De Beers Diamond Jewellers have set their own standards, both within the parameters of these criteria and moving beyond. Colour is not seen as a 'quality', but rather as a subjective characteristic, and while the majority of the diamonds selected sit between D and K, the brand also accepts exceptional diamonds within the D–Z colour range as long as the colours are pure, without tints of brown or grey. In terms of clarity, they work only within the range from FL (flawless) to SI2 (slight inclusions), so that the diamond looks clean to the naked eye.

Having established these criteria, and made their painstaking selection, De Beers Diamond Jewellers then continues the De Beers mentorship process of empowering the client through knowledge and understanding. It is important for clients to understand, appreciate and enjoy the difference in a De Beers diamond – to share in the whole selection and creative process. The De Beers Iris enables the client to do just this. By slowing down what the eye sees in a flash, the De Beers Iris, a moving light scan, allows the untrained eye to see the sparkle, brilliance and perfection of a De Beers diamond as if through the eyes of an industry expert, and to understand the concept of Fire, Life and Brilliance in real, visual terms. The Iris shows

the play of light through a diamond, illuminating the facets to create a kaleidoscope of moving light and shape. In a De Beers Diamond Jewellers diamond, the facets will light up at the same time, to the same intensity, showing that they are working perfectly and equally, building into an aesthetically pleasing kaleidoscopic form of absolute harmony that pays homage to the perfect balance and sacred geometry of nature. The De Beers Iris has become an essential and enjoyable part of the total De Beers Diamond Jewellers mentorship experience.

Two final touches are the ultimate guarantees of the integrity of these hand-chosen diamonds: the De Beers Marque; and the De Beers Passport, a counterfeit-proof certificate documenting every aspect of the purchase. The Marque, proprietary De Beers technology, is a microdot embedded with the brand name and a unique De Beers serial number; it is etched onto the table of all diamonds from 0.2 carats upwards. Invisible to the naked eye and impossible to remove or wipe off, it requires 250x magnification and can be seen by the client through the special De Beers Diamond Viewer, another unique facet of the total diamond experience. An effective security and identification measure, the Marque is cleverly positioned so as to be deep enough to catch the light and be seen under magnification, but also shallow enough not to compromise clarity, so that a flawless diamond with the De Beers Marque will still retain its GIA Flawless grading.

De Beers' diamond specialists fervently believe that the long quest for the diamond of your life may start with the 4 Cs but it shouldn't end there. This total diamond experience, the result of De Beers' own long journey, takes the search much further, delving into the personal relationship between the jeweller and the client, and between the client and the diamond. These relationships must encompass science and art, the rational and the instinctive, and mind and heart.

Opposite: De Beers Aura Ring with cushion-cut diamond, during and after the careful process of assemblage. *Previous pages:* Commissioned artwork exploring the Fire, Life and Brilliance of diamonds, graphite on paper, photographed with light dispersion, 2010.

SCULPTOR

De Beers–selected diamonds are cut for beauty. For beauty alone, sacrificing weight where necessary to obtain the Fire, Life and Brilliance, is the cornerstone of the brand's commitment to excellence. Traditionally, most diamonds, for obvious commercial considerations, are cut to maximise weight and minimise wastage. But De Beers Diamond Jewellers, guided by the high standards set for the brand by the team of world-renowned diamond experts at the De Beers Institute of Diamonds, decided to challenge conventions and put beauty and brilliance first, in order to reveal the full, radiant, inner light held within the heart of every diamond.

Diamond cutting is a true art form – near-mystical, meditative and metamorphic, alchemical in its process of transformation from rough crystal to light and life-filled treasure. Only a diamond can cut diamond. Through the centuries, cutting was seen as the key to fathoming the mysteries of the diamond, conquering the unconquerable, but in the earliest times, it was believed that the stone's magical power would be lost unless the diamond retained its natural state. In India, where cleaving may have originated some two thousand years ago, the natural octahedral shape was treasured for spiritual and religious reasons, a belief that persisted through the centuries so that the finest crystals were not traded but kept in India for emperors and Nizams, princes and rulers. Since naturally perfect octahedral diamonds are rare, rough stones would be fashioned to replicate the form. Traditionally, Indian diamonds were polished gently and subtly, using clarified butter and soft chamois leather, producing a soft, luminous lustre, preserving their natural forms. One of the many early diamond myths involves the cutting process, a challenge to the ancients, and the use, not of butter, but of goat's blood. In his *Naturalis Historia*, written in the first century A.D., Pliny stated that the diamond, the hardest material on earth, could only be cleaved and cut if first dipped in a he-goat's blood (the goat should also be fed on parsley and wine). There is a connection, if tenuous, since goat's blood was used for tempering iron, and steel knives hardened in this way were used to cleave diamonds. But the story, repeated through generations and across civilisations, could also have been part of the secrecy and superstition that has always surrounded the

THE CONSULTATION BY EXPERTS IN AMSTERDAM BEFORE THE GREAT STONE WAS CUT.

Photographs by favour of Messrs. Joseph Asscher & Co. and Messrs. M. J. Levy and Nephews, London.

diamond. Today, the secrecy and mystique continues, but with a more practical element, as the world's most revered diamond cutters have their own secret recipes for the abrasive diamond dust that is crucial to their art.

Diamond cutting developed in Europe in the Middle Ages, and appears to have been established as a trade first in Nuremberg, Germany, in 1375, and then, soon after, in Venice, Flanders and Paris, where the first documented diamond cutters were German immigrants. At first, in the fourteenth century, the diamonds were simply fashioned in rudimentary 'naïf' octahedral form, with a point and even, polished-flat surfaces, after which the point was truncated to form the table cut, and then the corners cut to form a lozenge shape. The pivotal concept of absolute symmetry in the positioning of facets is generally credited to the Flemish stonecutter Lodewyk van Bercken (Berquen) working in Bruges in 1475. His talent was nurtured by the jewel-loving Charles the Bold, Duke of Burgundy (1433–77), a devoted patron of the arts whose powerful domain encompassed Bruges with its flourishing diamond centre. Under Burgundy's patronage, diamond cutting evolved, becoming innovative and creative, and van Bercken is attributed with developing a rotary diamond-cutting and polishing wheel called a scaif, and inventing the pendeloque or briolette cut. He is said to have polished three great diamonds given to him by the Duke of Burgundy, one of which is reputed, by legend, to have been the Florentine, a pyramid-shaped yellow diamond that found its way into the possession of the Medici family in Florence.

The rose cut, or rosette, flat backed with broad triangular facets like an opening rosebud, became the most popular cut in the sixteenth century, although the hogback, a long narrow diamond with two sloping faceted sides and either a pointed ridge or a narrow table on the top, was used to form the petals of flowers or rosettes, crosses or letters of the alphabet, very often in religious IHS pendants (the monogram IHS being derived from the Greek word for Jesus). Eventually, while the rose cut reigned supreme through the seventeenth century, experiments coupled with advanced techniques bred the early brilliant cut, which appeared around 1690. This major development, revealing the diamond's true brilliance for the first time, had been encouraged by the patronage and influence in Paris of the Italian-born Cardinal Jules Mazarin (1602–1661), the powerful first Minister of the Crown, a passionate diamond devotee and collector who nurtured the art of diamond cutting. A more sophisticated version of the brilliant, a square shape with more facets, is generally attributed to a Venetian cutter named Peruzzi, although there is doubt that he even existed. It was during the seventeenth century that the great French merchant Jean-Baptiste Tavernier made his famous six voyages to the East, including India, visiting the Mughal court, witnessing and describing great, historic diamonds and bringing many of them back with him to the dazzling, diamond-adoring Sun King, Louis XIV. Tavernier's descriptions of stones such as the Great Mogul, a massive 280-carat, faceted, dome-shaped, greenish-blue diamond, apparently polished by a Venetian, gives an indication of the sophistication of diamond cutting at this time; the biggest and most important diamonds were given to the many European cutters who were installed at the Mughal court, in what may have been a mutual exchange of knowledge and skills, since cutting seems to have progressed at the same rate in India and Europe.

Versions of the brilliant cut continued to evolve, notably the cushion cut, a soft, rounded rectangle, while square and rose cuts were fashionable through the eighteenth century. With the industrialisation of the nineteenth century, steam-driven machinery helped to improve and refine the cutting operation, and various interpretations of the brilliant, along with what have come to be called 'old mine' cuts, illuminated nineteenth-century jewellery. However, the whole process of diamond cutting hit the headlines in the 1850s, when the audacious re-cutting of the historic Koh-i-Noor captured public imagination and became a major cultural event. The great Indian stone, one of the oldest known diamonds, with its long history of legends and blood-curdling adventure, was presented to Queen Victoria by the East India Company in 1848, when the Punjab was annexed by the British, coming under British rule. It was said that whoever owned the Koh-i-Noor ruled the world. When the majestic 186-carat stone was exhibited at the Great Exhibition in 1851, it was generally deemed dull, and Prince Albert in particular was disappointed with its lack of brilliance. Experienced cutters from Coster in Amsterdam were called in to re-cut the stone at Garrard, the Crown Jeweller, and, after long planning and deliberation, on 17 July 1852 the first facet was cut using a steam-driven scaif wielded by the Duke of Wellington, who had shown great interest in the project. The re-cutting process took thirty-eight days, leaving an oval brilliant of 108.93 carats that is now set into the Maltese cross at the front of the crown made in 1937 for H.M. Queen Elizabeth, the Queen Mother.

The dawn of the twentieth century ushered in a great new age of diamonds. A new influx of fine diamonds from South Africa, great technical progress, increased understanding of optics and the invention of tools, saws and lathes all conspired to take diamond cutting to an entirely new level of finesse and creativity. At the height of the Belle Époque, with its frenzied appetite for rare and valuable diamonds and its fashion for intensely white, slender and refined diamond and platinum jewels, a spectacularly monumental and magnificent rough diamond crystal of over three thousand carats was discovered in 1905, at the Premier Mine in South Africa, which had opened only two years previously. According to Lord Ian Balfour, renowned diamond historian, the discovery was 'one of the most momentous events in the entire history of gemstones'. Named after the Chairman of the Premier, Sir Thomas Cullinan, the diamond was, eventually, magnanimously presented to King Edward VII by General Botha, Prime Minister of the Transvaal, as a gift from his people to the King on his sixty-sixth birthday. The cutting of the diamond was entrusted to the firm of I.J. Asscher of Amsterdam, and the whole process was high-profile and highly complex, involving custom-made large tools and a specially constructed polishing room, thickly carpeted to prevent any breakage. It is said that the knife broke when the first

Following page, left: Cube (Pavilion Nocturne), a sculpture by Alberto Giacometti, 1933. *Following page, right: Untitled (Gem Painting),* acrylic and screen print on canvas by Luke Dowd, 2010.

cleaving blow was struck, but the massive stone was divided into two, and over a period of eight months, it was cut into nine diamonds. The largest, the Cullinan I at 530.20 carats, was renamed the Great Star of Africa and set into the Sceptre in the British Crown Jewels; Cullinan II, at 317.40 carats, was set into the British Imperial Crown; another was given by Edward VII to Queen Alexandra; and the other major diamonds were presented to the Princess of Wales, later Queen Mary, and are now part of the jewels of Queen Elizabeth II, affectionately known as Granny's Chips.

With more attention than ever focused on the diamond, experimentation, research and improved skills led to the development in 1919 of the modern brilliant cut with fifty-eight facets – thirty-three above and twenty-five below (including the culet). Such carefully plotted proportions and symmetry unleashed far more fire and brilliance than had yet been revealed in any diamond. The new brilliant or 'ideal' cut as it was known was the creation of a young Belgian mathematician, engineer and physicist, Marcel Tolkowsky, whose family, of Russian origin, were successful diamond cutters in Antwerp. Tolkowsky set out to define the ideal proportions for a round brilliant diamond with maximum brilliance and light dispersion, and in 1919 he wrote a master's thesis setting out his ideal proportions and explaining how the light worked in a diamond with these dimensions. His calculations set the standard for modern diamond cuts, creating a model that has continued to evolve, improve and innovate over the past century. Today, a high degree of skill is involved in achieving the perfect brilliant cut, aided by modern technology, including lasers and computer optics. The round brilliant remains the classic cut; all others are termed 'fancy' cuts, and include, for example, the baguette, beloved of the twenties and thirties and then again fashionable in the fifties; the pointed oval navette or marquise, popular in the sixties and seventies; the elegant emerald cut; the soft oval; the scintillating noble briolette; the geometric square; and more modern cuts such as the princess, Asscher, or radiant cut.

At De Beers Diamond Jewellers today, diamonds are all about brilliance. De Beers Diamond Jewellers raises the bar further than ever before, selecting what they consider to be the best diamonds in the world, those that have been impeccably cut to show the key attributes of Fire, Life and Brilliance to perfection. Each diamond has superb proportions and unerring symmetry with the minute critical angles between facets executed with the utmost precision. All the light entering the diamond must return back to the eye of the onlooker, stimulating the brain and stirring the heart. If the cutter changes the optimum angles of a diamond, even fractionally, light will leak and brilliance will be compromised. Equally, there has to be no sacrifice of dispersion, so that the white light is sliced into shards of rainbow glints, the colours of the spectrum, in perpetual motion, shimmering with every slight movement, creating visual excitement. On paper, two diamonds might appear to be identical, with identical qualities or classifications, yet De Beers diamond experts are able to see the difference in transparency, light, brilliance, beauty and personality, comparable to the difference between mountain and pond water. Even more important and moving beyond the most stringent quantifiable classifications, the De Beers Diamond Jewellers diamond is chosen, with dedication and passion, for beauty, individuality and harmony, with the expert eye of a master sculptor, an eye that sees into the very soul of the divine diamond.

Previous page, left: Diamond cutter from I.J. Asscher of Amsterdam working on the division of the great Cullinan Diamond. *Previous page, right:* Photomontage illustrating the division of the Cullinan Diamond. *Following pages:* Annabel Oval-Cut Diamond Ring set in platinum, starting from carat weights of 2.0. DB Classic Solitaire with emerald-cut diamond set in platinum, starting from carat weights of 0.50. DB Classic Solitaire with round brilliant-cut diamond set in platinum, starting from carat weights of 0.20. DB Classic Solitaire with pear-cut diamond set in platinum, starting from carat weights of 1.0. DB Classic Solitaire with cushion-cut diamond set in platinum, starting from carat weights of 1.0.

Opposite: Construct X-B, a
Polaroid by Barbara Kasten,
1981, courtesy of Carl Freedman
Gallery, London.

"Diamond cutting is a true art form, near-mystical, meditative and metamorphic, alchemical in its process of transformation from rough crystal to light and life-filled treasure."

"The diamond, once representing a social divide, has become socially inclusive, accessible, desirable to all generations and ages, worn for day or night, formal or casual, classic or sporty, the most powerful expression of individual style."

Opposite: Artist's impression of light flowing from a diamond, gouache on paper, 2010.

FIRE

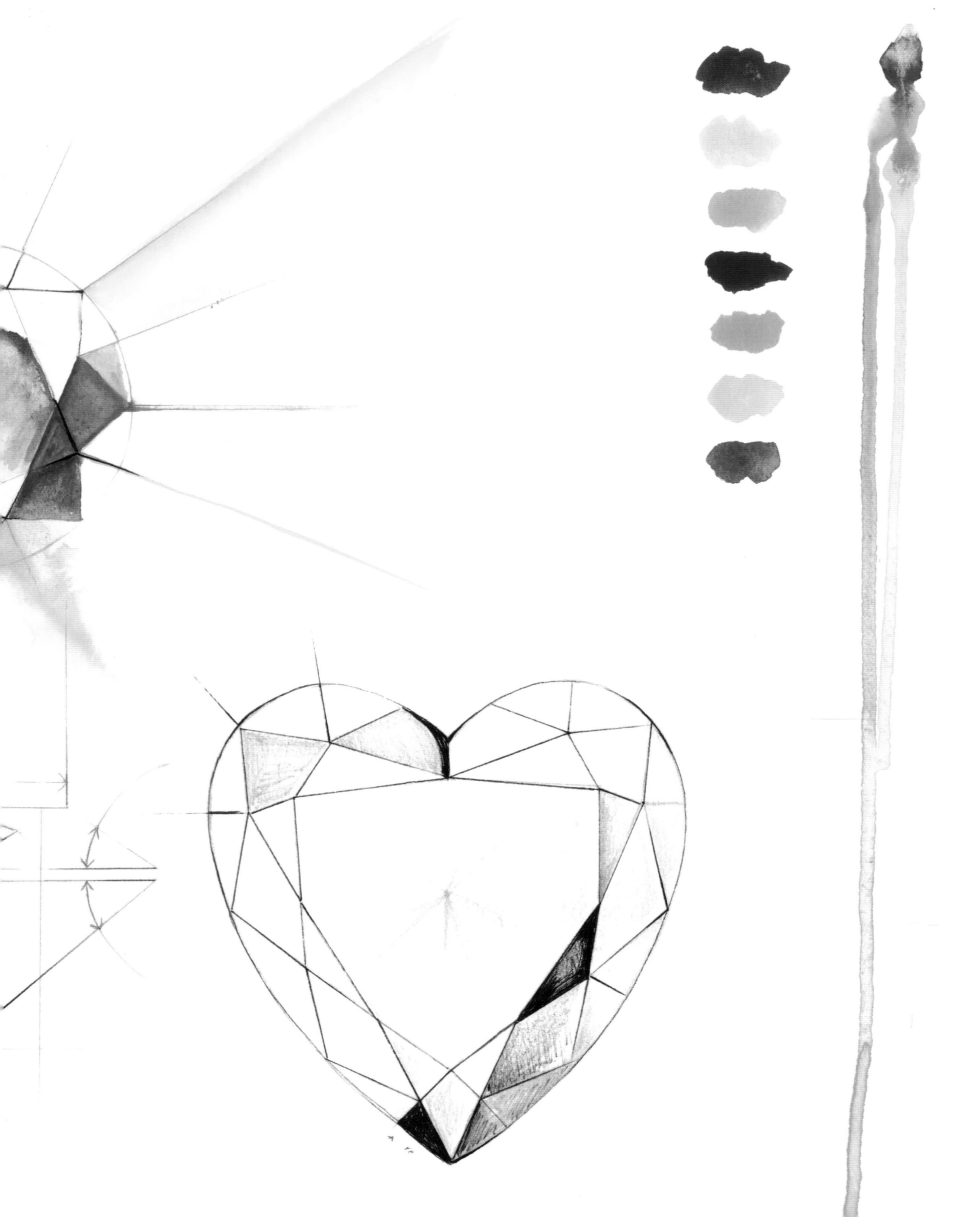

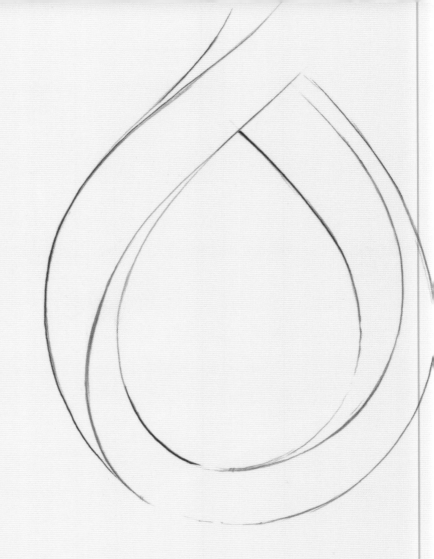

LIFE

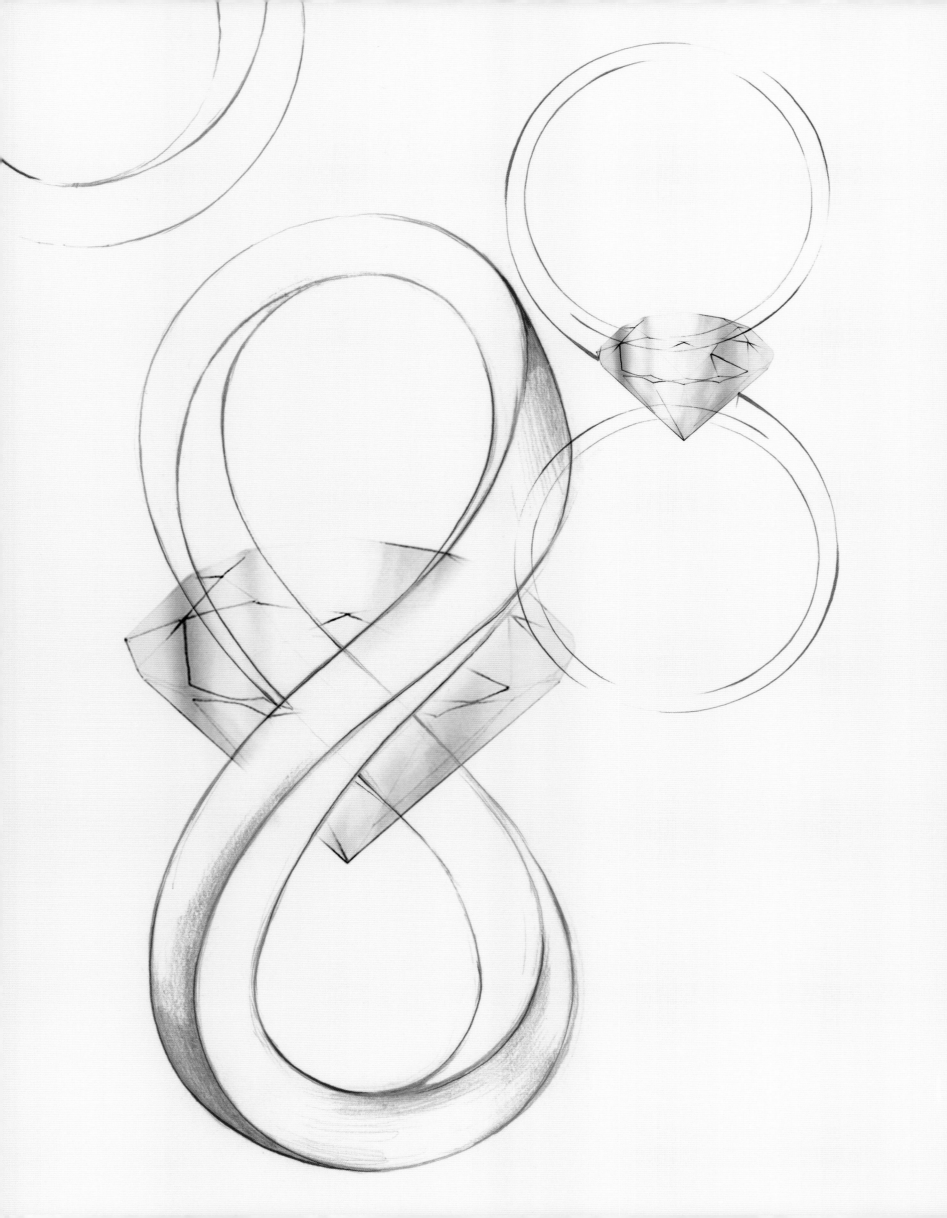

BRILLIANCE

COLOUR AND CHARACTER

Each and every diamond has its own personality. Shy or strong, introverted or extroverted – a diamond's character unfolds from within its infinite depths and reflections. And for those who know how to listen, each diamond has its own story to tell. More than anyone, De Beers Diamond Jewellers knows how to listen. They revel in these stories, celebrating the diversity and individual character of each diamond. As one of De Beers' experts with forty years of experience states: 'It is impossible for two diamonds to be the same'. This is the essence of the De Beers Difference.

Perhaps the strongest characters of all belong to coloured diamonds, the ravishing rarities of the gemstone world, nature's masterpieces, each intensely individual, expressive, engaging and, on occasion, even fascinatingly eccentric. As the famous mineralogist and father of crystallography René Just Haüy wrote in 1817, 'Gemstones are the flowers of the mineral world, and the fancy coloured diamond is the orchid'.

It is said that for every natural coloured diamond there are some ten thousand colourless specimens, and it is this extreme rarity, the mesmerising miracle of its creation, along with an emotive beauty and hypnotic magnetism, that have turned the coloured diamond into the superstar of the precious jewellery world. The coloured diamond takes the client into the realm of cultivated connoisseurship, answering today's rampant quest for the ultimate in one-of-a-kind individuality: the near unattainable. Usually small and subtle, discreet and unassuming, the coloured diamond possesses a sophisticated, low-key glamour, whispering its message of personal style and discerning educated taste, recognised only by other elite connoisseurs and diamond aficionados. It is the pinnacle of new luxury.

The appreciation of the coloured diamond as a jewel is a relatively recent phenomenon. For many years, the fancy coloured diamond was considered more of a scientific curiosity, a glass-case specimen, a fluke of nature, largely unrelated to jewellery, while shades of brown, grey, beige, even pale pink, were overlooked as rejects. But over the past decade

Pages 101-105: Artist's impression of the Fire, Life and Brilliance of De Beers diamonds, gouache, pencil and collage on paper, 2010.

or two, interest in coloured diamonds has escalated to fever pitch, grabbing the limelight with astronomic prices at auctions in London, New York and Hong Kong, leading avid, sophisticated collectors on a frenetic global treasure hunt for the ultra-precious, ultra-rare, truly unique diamond. Great interest was sparked early on in the current craze when deposits of heavenly, sugar-pink diamonds were discovered in the Argyle Mine in the late seventies and eighties. Glorious, sun-coloured yellow diamonds from South Africa or South America drifted onto the horizon in the eighties. De Beers Diamond Jewellers has been instrumental in disseminating this burgeoning desire; but while generally the focus has been on the top classifications of 'vivid' or 'intense', once again De Beers draws on its innate, in-depth understanding of the diamond and years of world-class expertise, to look beyond the quantifiable, beyond the mainstream, to slowly reveal one of the remaining secrets of the gem world: coloured diamonds in sublimely subtle, often indefinable shades and nuances of tone. These are poetic diamonds of great charisma, selected with passion, intuition and an expert eye, in colours that seem to crystallise the mists of time and encapsulate the warmth of the sun on the earth, a captivating palette of soft shadowy smoke grey, powdery metallic blue, mellow ochre, jonquil fading into moss green, warm taupe, fiery chestnut, orangy pink and purplish pink like slivers of sunset. With these meltingly tender diamonds that fall outside of the established grading system, De Beers Diamond Jewellers continues on its mission to explore the natural diversity of diamonds, to reveal their beauty and release their emotions. Prized as works of art, such diamonds, each hand-chosen for its individuality and poetry, are framed in timeless designs and honoured with exquisite craftsmanship. The Talisman Collection, with its sophisticated barbarism, was conceived as an homage to nature, studded proudly with rough, coloured diamonds, sugary rocks, in earth tones resonating with enchantment – a reminder of the earliest role of the diamond as magical amulet. The Swan Lake Collection, with its alluring flow of gentle colour, plays with captivating harmonies of tone and translucency.

Opposite: Neon, Clear Ruby, and Blue Coated Turquoise Pumped Blue, unique Cibachrome by Rob and Nick Carter, 2003, courtesy of Fine Art Society, London.

The coloured diamond is unrivalled in the world of gems for bringing together the fire and brilliance, the dispersion, refraction and scintillation of the king of gemstones with exquisitely refined and provocatively mysterious colours: cherry blossom candy pinks, baby blues, gooseberry and olive greens, liquid golden and canary yellows, cognac browns and sparkling champagnes, each with its own spectrum of subtle tones and nuances. These colours are unfathomable and unpredictable; nature always has the last word. The industry grading system orders colours in degrees of intensity, starting with vivid at the top, as the most desirable, through intense, fancy and light. However, the coloured diamond cannot be pigeonholed or categorized in an exact scientific way, and many have a dominant colour and a modifier or secondary colour, as in orange pink, or purple pink, so that there are seemingly endless permutations of tones. Assessing coloured diamonds is an entirely subjective exercise, demanding a special level of understanding, sensibility and experience. It is about the intensity and subtlety of the three components of colour – hue, tone and saturation – and the way they play with light, interacting with the fire and brilliance of the diamond. Just as De Beers Diamond Jewellers selects and cuts diamonds to its own exacting standards, opting for beauty and brilliance above all, so they choose coloured diamonds according to an acute, painterly sensitivity, using refined taste and a discerning appreciation of the gem's subtleties of beauty and rarity. This too is part of the De Beers Difference.

The story of the creation of coloured diamonds is an integral part of their fascination; added to the already extraordinary formation process, their journey through millions of years, from deep in the earth's core to its surface, is the random interaction or interchange of trace elements with their carbon make-up, or the equally random changes wrought by tremendous heat and pressure that distort atomic structure. Yellow diamonds, like brilliant sunlight, fresh, contemporary and found mainly in South Africa and Australia, are the result of nitrogen in the crystal. Less than one percent of diamonds are yellow. The Eureka, the first diamond discovered in South Africa, was a pale yellow. Blue diamonds are formed when boron is present; violet when hydrogen is in the carbon mix. Green diamonds are created when natural radiation (completely harmless) impacts a formed diamond after the crystallization process, over millions of years. Pink, red (the rarest), purple and brown diamonds (the most plentiful), in a plethora of shades, like cognac, honey and peach, are formed by enormous heat and pressure deep in the earth, compressing and distorting the atomic lattice.

Coloured diamonds have been known and treasured throughout history, the combination of colour and light enhancing their magic and mystique. Hindus reserved different colours of diamonds for the four different castes, with Brahmins awarded the finest colourless stones, compared to rock crystal or the moon (in the *Agastimata*, sixth century A.D.); brown for the warriors, the Kshatriya; pale yellow or cream-coloured specimens for the Vaisyas (landowners); and grey or black diamonds were assigned to servants. Among the legendary Golconda diamonds, the inimitable deep sapphire blue Hope Diamond, once part of the French Crown Jewels but known as much for its alleged curse as for its rare and magnificent beauty, is arguably, after the Koh-i-Noor, the most famous diamond in the world. The pink Agra was given to Babur, the first Mughal Emperor (1483–1530), in gratitude for lives spared during the battle for Agra. The Florentine, a pale citron yellow, came into the possession of the Medici family of Florence and was seen by Tavernier in the collection of the Grand Duke of Tuscany, in 1657, but disappeared with the last Austrian Emperor. The Dresden Green, a true deep green pear-shaped diamond, unique among famous gems, was owned by Frederick Augustus II (1733–63), ruler of Saxony. It was originally mounted in an Order of the Golden Fleece and then in a hat ornament, which now is a highlight of the treasures on display in the Grünes Gewölbe collection in Dresden. In more recent times, the Heart of Eternity, a dark fancy vivid blue 27.64-carat heart-shaped diamond, was part of the De Beers Millennium Jewels collection, on display in 2000 in the Millennium Dome.

Colour is undoubtedly a powerful emotional key to a jewel, and while even the smallest coloured diamond has a strong personality and presence, De Beers' diamond experts are driven to nurture a strong emotional engagement with all their diamonds, searching for

Following page, left: De Beers Millennium Blue Diamonds, reproduced at approximately life size. *Following page, right: Untitled (Millennium Star)*, a mixed-media collage by Luke Dowd. The De Beers Millennium Star, of which this is a portrait, is a 'D' colour, internally and externally flawless pear-shaped diamond, cut to perfect proportions, weighing 203.04 carats. It is the second largest faceted D-Flawless diamond in the world. The 273.15-carat Centenary Diamond is the largest.

character and charisma in every one, coloured or colourless. They understand the emotional response sparked by a particular diamond; they believe the reaction to a diamond is like falling in love, starting with the all-important *coup de foudre*, an instinctive attraction, then deepening into a bond, a relationship; the diamond becomes a part of the wearer's persona. Different people are attracted to different diamonds, and it is important for the client to listen to that initial instinctive reaction stirred by the visual excitement of a diamond. As one of the leading experts at the De Beers Institute of Diamonds explains, 'The eye, brain and heart measure the qualities of a diamond in a flash, producing an emotional reaction that a client should trust'. There is a perfect diamond for everybody; De Beers Diamond Jewellers believes firmly that the diamond chooses you. Their mission is to enable this process, helping clients find their own true diamond love.

As with coloured diamonds, a client may be drawn to a particular diamond that, on paper, is not necessarily the best or most rare. Yet one diamond will somehow call to them. De Beers Diamond Jewellers believes it is about moving beyond the formulaic criteria of the established '4 Cs'. Rather, it is an individual search for true beauty. For this reason, De Beers' experts choose diamonds of character, irrespective of classification: large diamonds of lower colour grade but with extraordinary brilliance; or a small diamond with a compelling intensity that adds to its exquisite perfection. The combination of Fire, Life and Brilliance is different in every diamond. De Beers Diamond Jewellers introduces the client to the whole universe of diamonds.

In this way, De Beers Diamond Jewellers is blazing a trail, leading the way forward in introducing an entirely new dimension to the appreciation of the diamond: an aesthetic, even poetic element that sees and understands the diamond as a true and wondrous work of art. One of the pioneers of this approach at the De Beers Institute of Diamonds defines this new dimension: 'The new rarity is visible beauty, in any colour or quality'. The new rarity is also size, as gem-quality diamonds of over three carats have become increasingly scarce.

Opposite: Swan Lake Necklace with fancy-cut yellow, orange and pink diamonds set in white, pink and yellow gold, total weight 34.5 carats.

But more important than this is the fact that De Beers Diamond Jewellers, believing in the rarity of size, defies convention to offer larger diamonds, selected according to their own exemplary standards of beauty and brilliance, in a range of warm white colours (J, K, L). This means that De Beers is continually able to surprise and delight clients by showing them a diamond, of great character, that is double the size they thought they wanted or could afford by following the 4 Cs rigidly. These large, imposing diamonds may be less rare than colourless diamonds, but not of lower quality, or less brilliant or beautiful.

The role model for contemporary diamonds, in terms of both size and beauty, remains the magnificent Millennium Star: the flagship De Beers Diamond Jewellers diamond and the first diamond acquired for the newly created brand. This mesmerising diamond, cut according to the new De Beers Diamond Jewellers criteria for beauty, provides the inspiration for all De Beers diamonds.

The Millennium Star, a pear-shaped diamond of 203.04 carats, with fifty-four facets, D colour and flawless clarity, was the centrepiece of the unique collection of diamonds called the De Beers Millennium Jewels. The 777 carat rough – the sixth-biggest gem-quality diamond ever found – was discovered by an alluvial digger in the early nineties in what is now the Democratic Republic of Congo. It was purchased by De Beers and kept for the Millennium celebrations: a suitable monument to time, calm perfection in the chaos of nature, a drop of precious permanence at a time, and in a world, of change. The cutting process took three years and required a special cutting room and special tools, as well as complex planning involving some hundred models, to maximise the potential of the rough and obtain a polished result of immense beauty. A former chairman of De Beers proclaimed it the most beautiful diamond he had ever seen. The Millennium Star, in its full glory, set in a lyrical Grasslands Necklace, became the star jewel at the launch of De Beers Diamond Jewellers in 2001 – a symbol of brilliance, beauty and charisma.

Opposite: 030, a photograph by James Welling, 2006, courtesy of Maureen Paley, London.

YELLOW

Opposite: A selection of rough yellow diamonds. Image courtesy of the De Beers Group Archives.

PINK

BLUE

Opposite: A selection of rough blue diamonds. Image courtesy of the De Beers Group Archives.

"This country is a completely new subject for me; I'll need a palette of diamonds and precious stones."

CLAUDE MONET TO THÉODORE DURET,
BORDIGHERA, FEBRUARY 2, 1884

Opposite: I don't want to get over you, a photograph by Wolfgang Tillmans, 2000, courtesy of Maureen Paley, London. *Following page, left:* The Making of the Swan Lake Collection: Finishing the settings of the Swan Lake Necklace. *Following page, right:* Artworks from the De Beers sketchbook for the Swan Lake Collection.

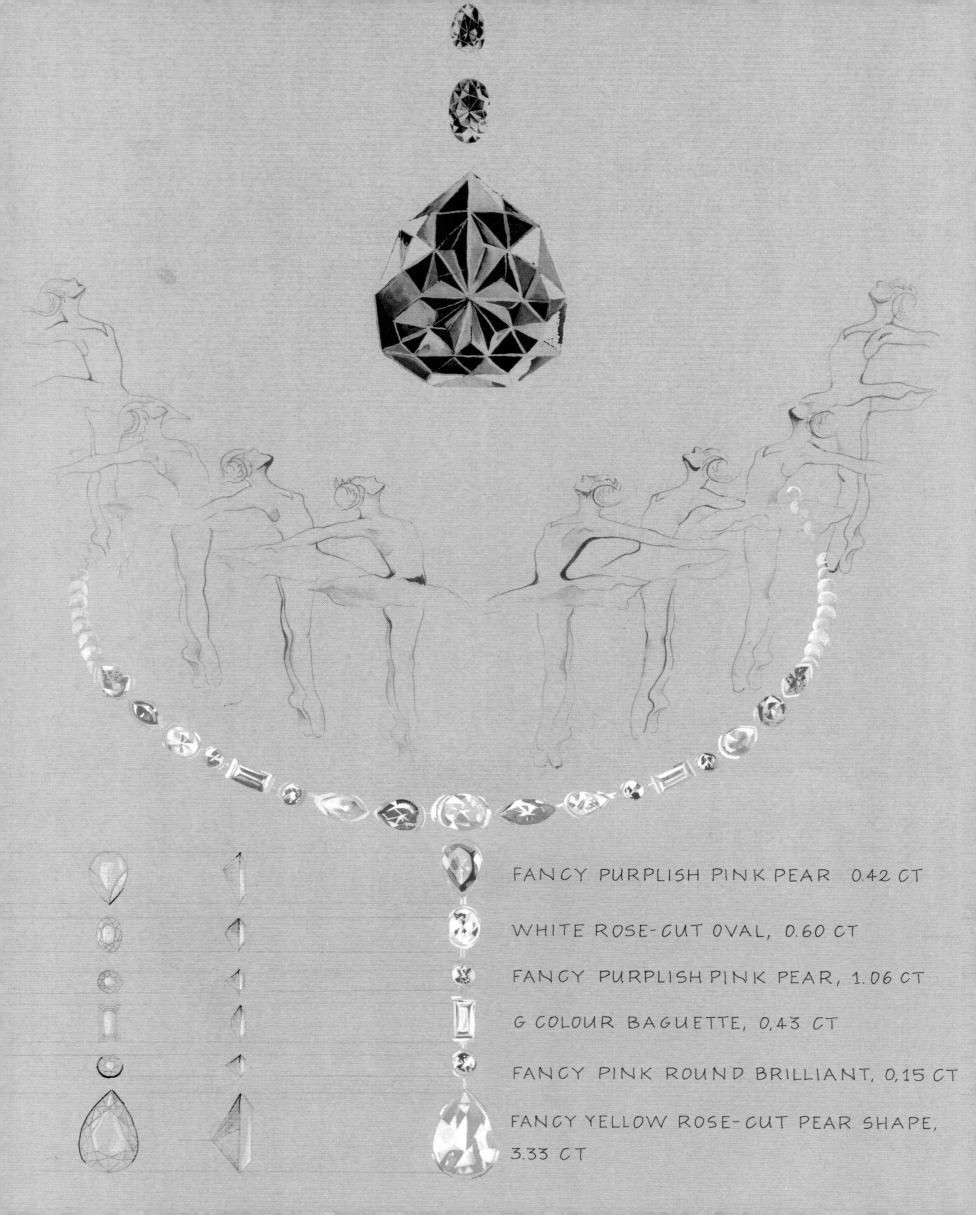

FANCY PURPLISH PINK PEAR 0.42 CT

WHITE ROSE-CUT OVAL, 0.60 CT

FANCY PURPLISH PINK PEAR, 1.06 CT

G COLOUR BAGUETTE, 0,43 CT

FANCY PINK ROUND BRILLIANT, 0,15 CT

FANCY YELLOW ROSE-CUT PEAR SHAPE,
3.33 CT

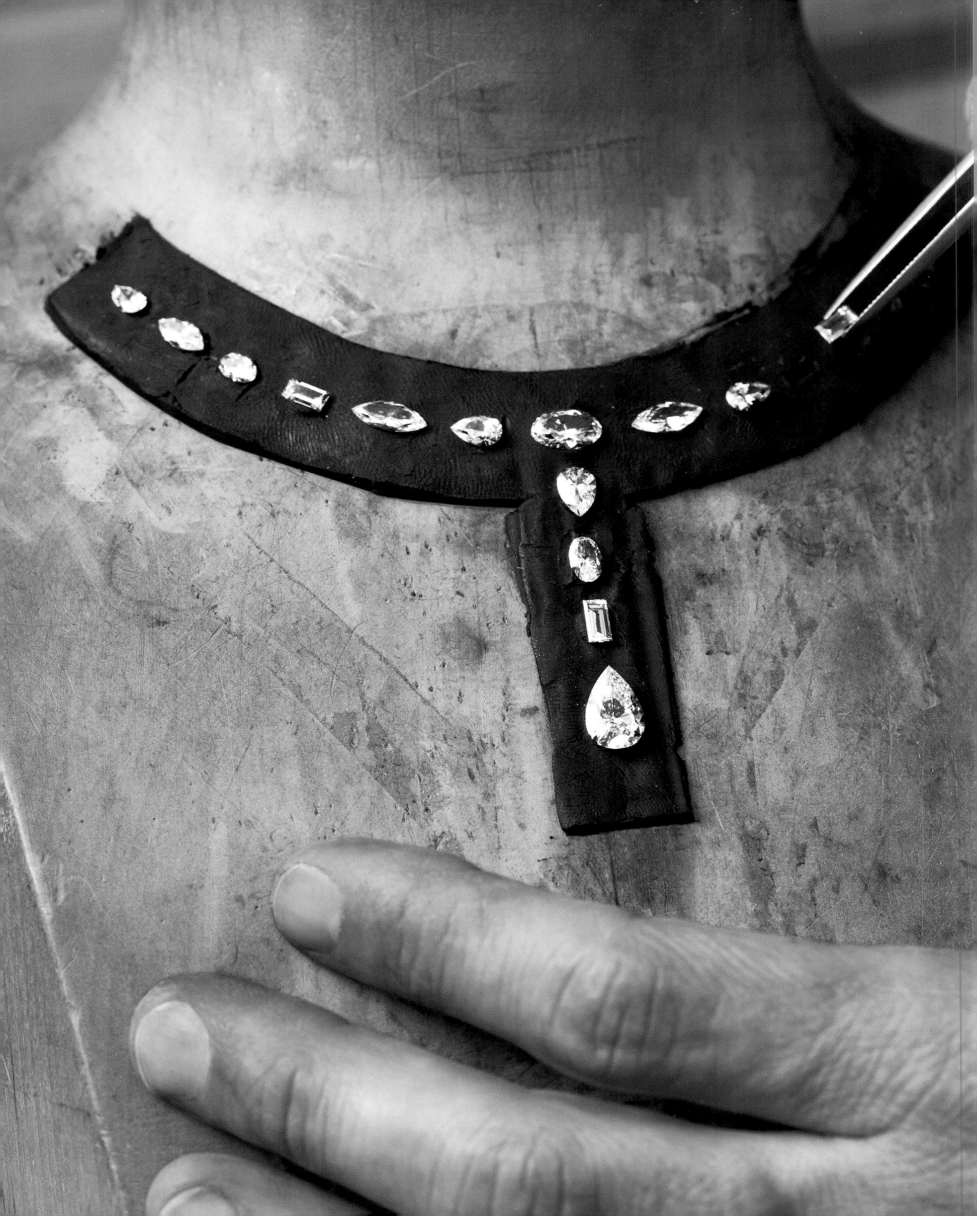

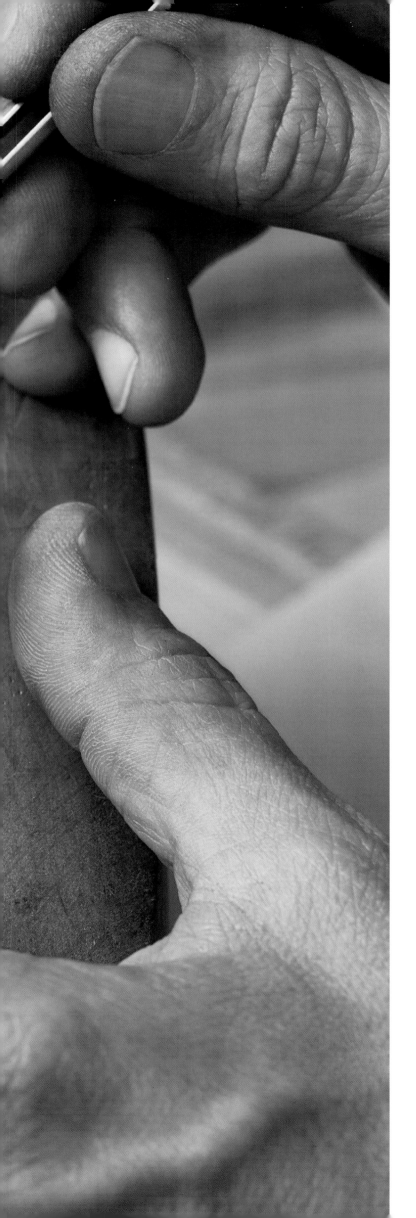

" The simple pure lines and form of the Swan Lake Collection allow the diamond to shine supreme. "

" Diamonds make women look and feel good; diamonds cut through styles and across generations. "

Previous page, left: The Making of the Swan Lake Collection: Assembling the Swan Lake Necklace.
Previous page, right: The Making of the Swan Lake Collection: A De Beers diamond jeweller crafting the settings for the Swan Lake Necklace. *Opposite:* The Making of the Swan Lake Collection: Positioning the diamonds for the White Swan Lake Necklace.

"The diamond, a repository of all geometry, an inner force reflecting the seven colours of the iris."

PAUL CLAUDEL

"As one of the leading experts at the De Beers Institute of Diamonds explains, 'The eye, brain and heart measure the qualities of a diamond in a flash, producing an emotional reaction that a client should trust.

Opposite: Lords of Kolbojnik, mixed media on canvas by Tal R, 2002, courtesy of Contemporary Fine Arts, Berlin.

"A unique objet d'art, the monumental circular gold shield or medallion is embedded with 691 diamonds, totalling 271 carats in weight, with an extraordinary centre rough diamond of over 17 carats."

"The diamond chooses you."

Opposite: The Talisman Wonder weighs two pounds (approximately 907 grams) and measures 18 centimetres in diameter. It features 691 diamonds set in 18K white gold for a total carat weight of 271. Among them: a centre rough diamond, total weight over 17 carats; 110 rough diamonds, total weight almost 160 carats; 9 rose-cut cognac-coloured diamonds, total weight 3 carats; 19 polished round diamonds, total weight approximately 5 carats; 146 brilliant white diamonds, total weight 36 carats; and 406 polished white baguettes, total weight almost 50 carats. *Following page, left:* The Making of the Talisman Wonder: Polishing the settings for the diamonds. *Following page, right:* The Making of the Talisman Wonder: Setting the diamonds.

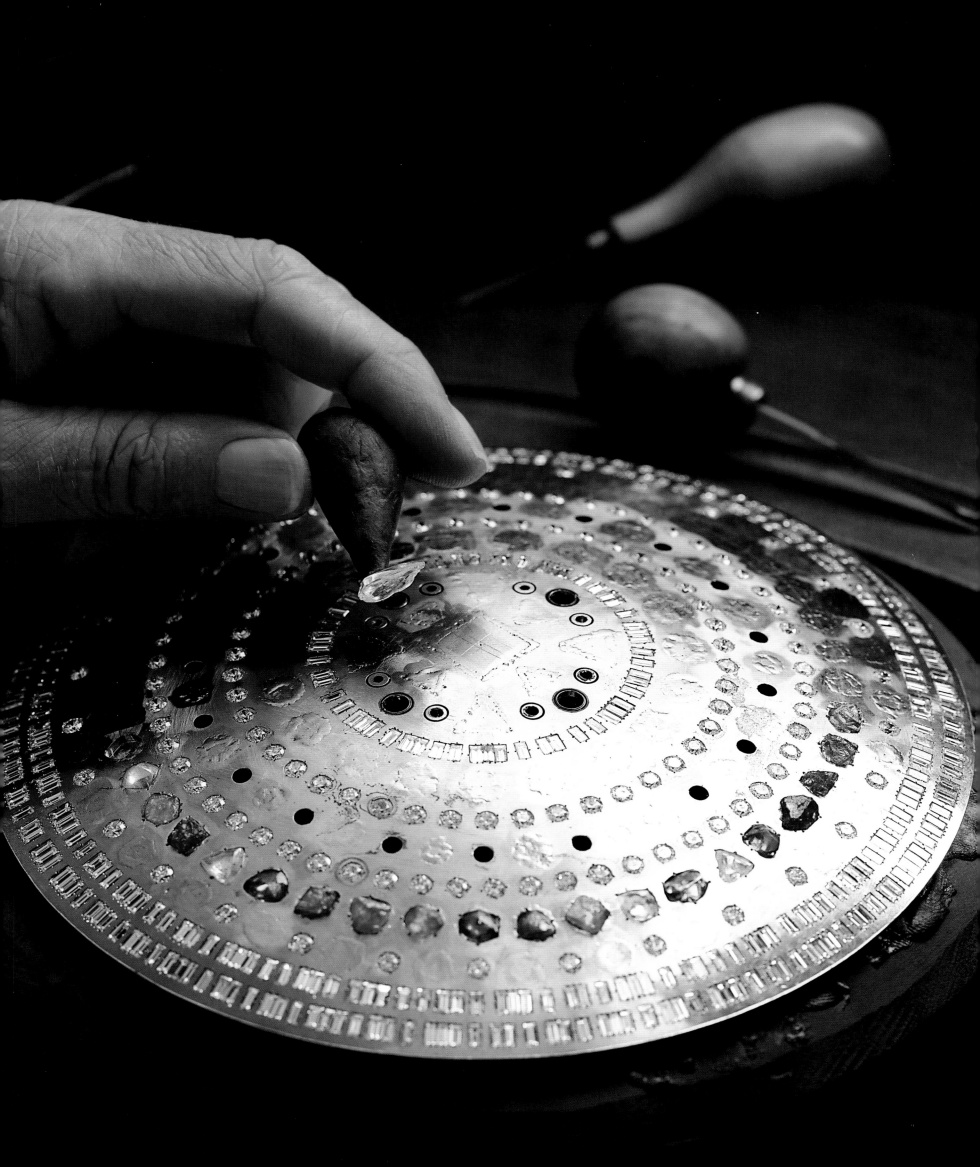

TIMELESS

For a jewel to be truly timeless, it has to capture and hold its moment in time. De Beers Diamond Jewellers captures the mood of the moment by fusing the essential timelessness of the diamond with dynamic contemporary design, touched with iconoclastic verve and modern romance. Backed by expertise and experience, De Beers understands the rules well enough to break them. Barrier-breaking creative concepts are brought to life by craftsmanship that combines tradition with inventive ingenuity, centuries-old skills of hand-workmanship with cutting-edge virtuosity. Dedicated to innovation in both artistry and craftsmanship, exploring new frontiers and pushing boundaries, De Beers Diamond Jewellers' design team melds the diamond's noble heritage with its natural beauty and ageless modernity. Aeons old yet eternally young, the diamond remains the ultimate jewellery classic.

Each day De Beers designers must ask the question: What is classic? Classic is the starting point, the basis and reference for all De Beers Diamond Jewellers design. But what does classic mean today? Women proudly buy their own diamonds, both to add a spark of brilliance to their personal style and express their individuality, and to enrich their lives with a precious, intimate treasure, to cherish and keep close to them, all day, every day. How does one renew and reinvigorate, celebrate and perpetuate the timeless mystique of the diamond, to encapsulate its dream in a jewel that will appeal to these women of today?

De Beers Diamond Jewellers believes the answer is to bring a new soul and enchantment to classicism. To design jewels that embrace the universal appeal and meaning of the diamond, jewels layered with legend and loaded with symbols that speak a global language, telling stories of enchantment and eternity. Designs that pay homage to the eternal feminine.

The diamond itself, hand-chosen for its unique De Beers Fire, Life and Brilliance, is always the starting point for a De Beers Diamond Jewellers design. The divine diamond inspires and stimulates creative visions. Concepts are developed to enhance the radiance of the diamond, to act as a conduit between the energy and sparkle of the diamond and its wearer, in the manner

Following pages: Traveling Still, Half Moon Bay, a photograph by Rob Carter, 2010.

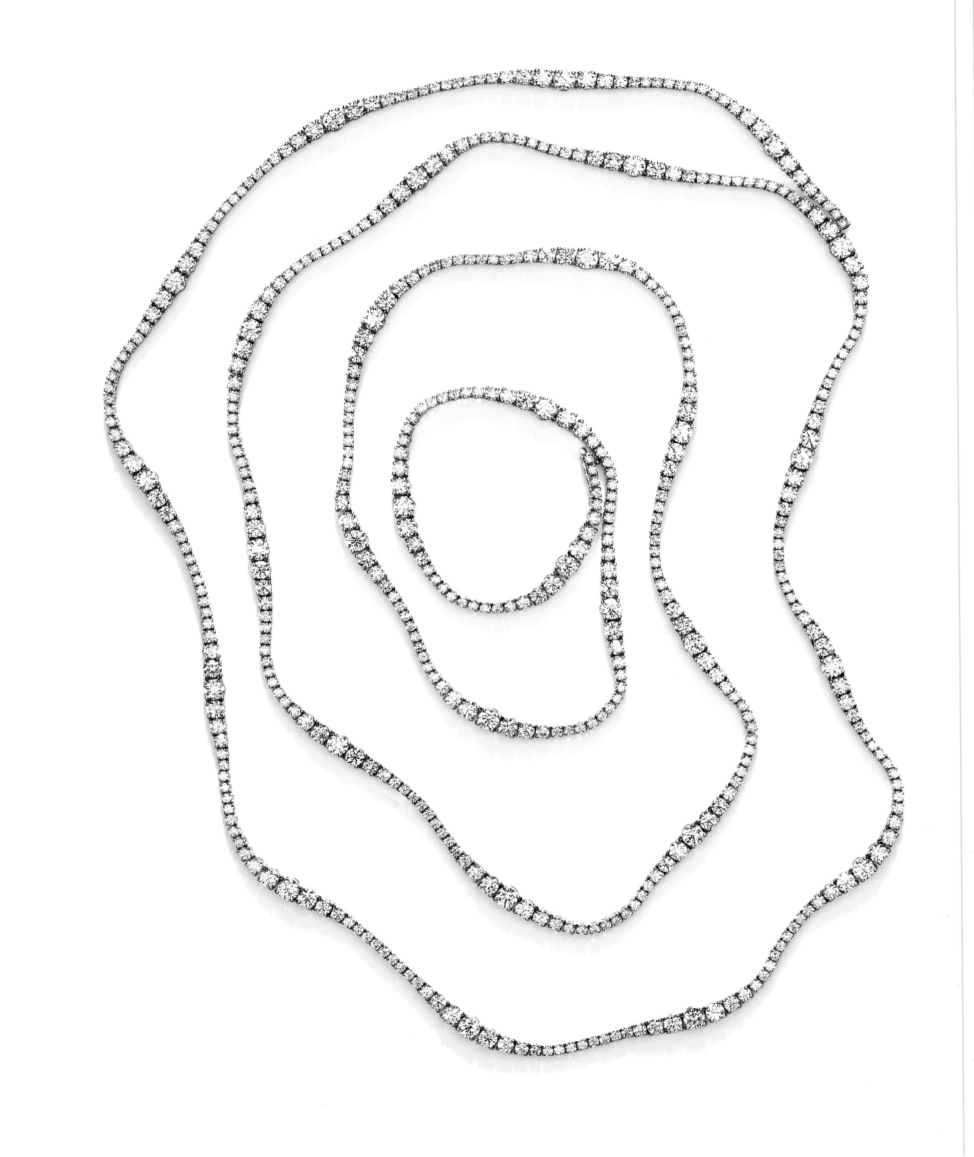

of an ancient talisman; the light and brilliance, the power and dynamism of the diamond are almost magically transferred to the wearer. Settings are designed to slowly reveal the beauty of the diamond, its luminous secrets and infinite depths. While the diamond is always hero of the jewel, elegant sophistication is woven around it through harmony of line, form and exquisite details – silky threads of micropavé work or emblematic motifs, a love-knot, a flower.

Each diamond is a miracle and microcosm of nature, its perfection and chaos. Nature has been a perennial influence and inspiration at De Beers Diamond Jewellers, starting with Wildflowers, one of the creative concepts to launch the brand in 2002. From the start, the Wildflowers Collection showed how De Beers Diamond Jewellers, always working against the grain of entrenched conventions and diamond clichés, takes an unexpected, unsentimental view of nature. Inspired by humble wildflowers found only in the South African wilderness, light and lively with lush asymmetric abandon and delicate dancing movement, the jewels have evolved and grown to be iconic De Beers interpretations of floral themes. The Lily Collection symbolised femininity, royalty and fresh beginnings, its style touched by the wayward glamour of the twenties.

The Enchanted Lotus Collection links the diamond with the lotus flower, both ancient, universal symbols of purity, serenity and eternity. Both grow out of darkness, the diamond in the earth's core, the lotus in muddy waters, moving towards the light to reveal beauty and perfection. The lotus, revered in Eastern cultures, is associated with the soul, rebirth and enlightenment. In the Enchanted Lotus, the stylised outline of the flower is traced in impeccably crafted fine trails of micropavé-set diamonds that twist into a heart framing the lotus. The Lotus and Atea designs, intricately lace-like, are made modern by their interplay of volume and lightness, with lines of light moving in space, the diamonds floating on the skin, shimmering in their ribbons of fine white gold.

Previous page, left: Lines Necklace with 480 diamonds set in white gold, total carat weight 51.18. *Previous page, right:* Lines Necklace with 480 diamonds set in white gold, total carat weight 51.18. *Opposite:* Enchanted Lotus Large Ring with 0.30-carat round brilliant-cut diamond, total carat weight 1.11. Enchanted Lotus Large Pendant with 0.30-carat centre diamond, total carat weight 0.90. Enchanted Lotus Brooch with 0.40-carat round brilliant-cut diamond, total carat weight 1.47. Enchanted Lotus Sleeper Earrings, total carat weight 0.45. Enchanted Lotus Band set in white gold, total carat weight 1.31. Enchanted Lotus Small Studs, total carat weight 0.15. Enchanted Lotus Large Studs, total carat weight 0.44.

"On paper, two diamonds might appear to be identical, with identical qualities or classifications, yet De Beers experts are able to see the difference in transparency, light, brilliance, beauty and personality, comparable to the difference between mountain and pond water."

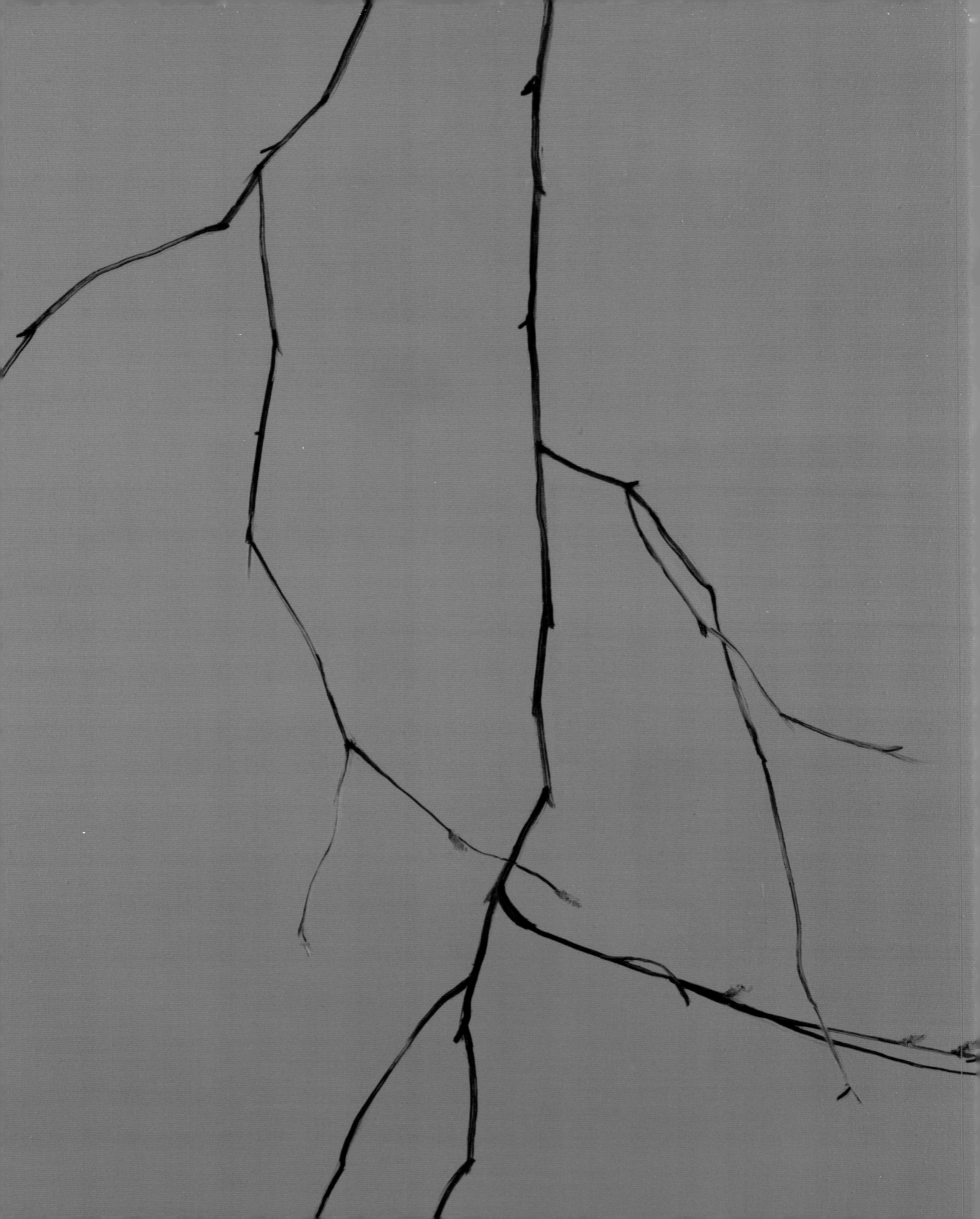

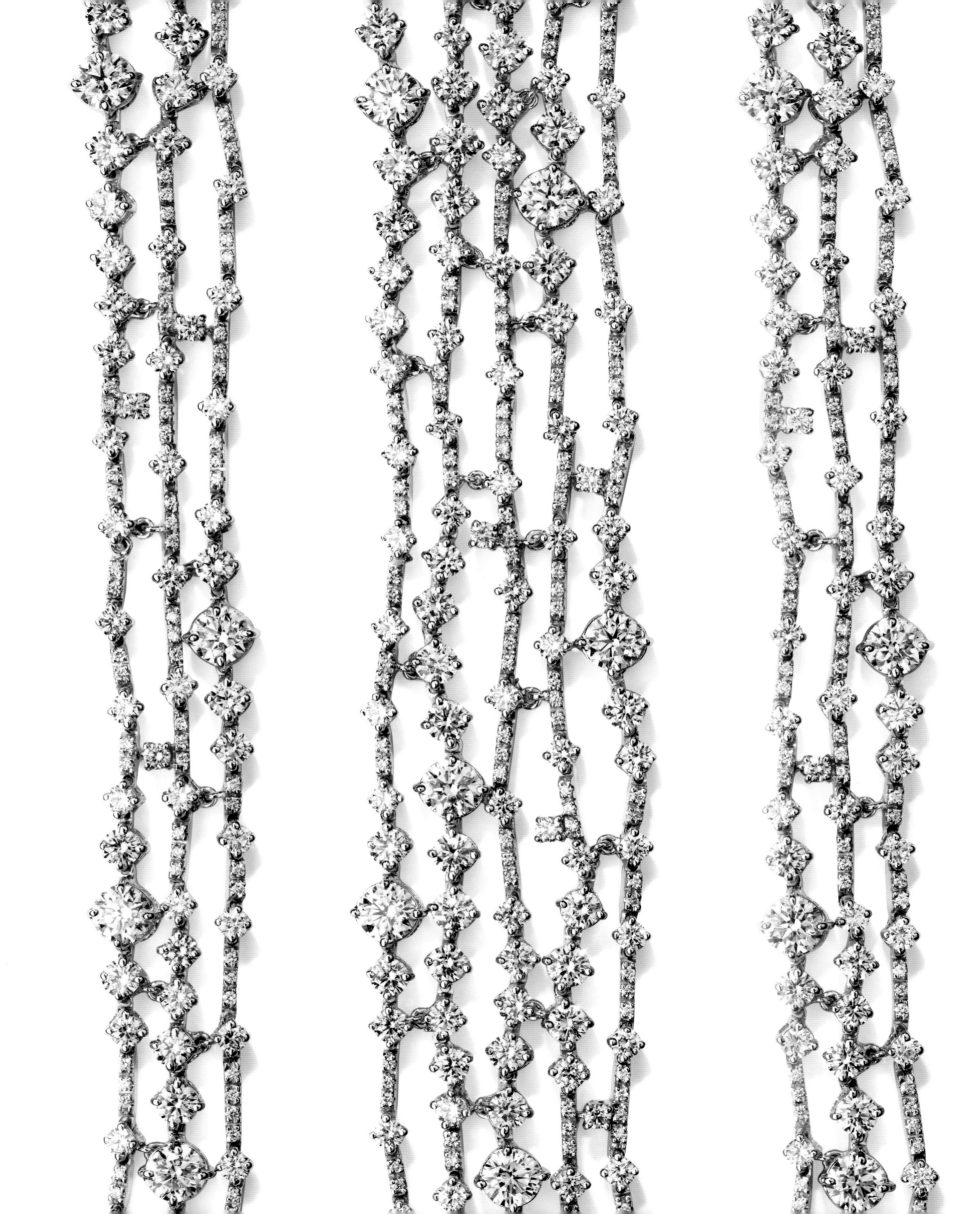

Water, like the diamond, is one of nature's most precious resources, and designs depicting water show De Beers diamond jewellery's characteristic lightness and fluidity to perfection. Diamonds become single drops or cascades of liquid light, as in the dewdrops of the Reverie Celebration Bands, or in the dramatic Princess Lea Necklace, with its magnificent drop- or pear-shaped diamonds, hung within a waterfall of diamonds. The Princess Lea, composed entirely of superb quality D colour, internally flawless diamonds, is a modern masterpiece, with an aristocratic air, that took some twelve-hundred hours of highly skilled artisanship to create. It is the showpiece of the Lea Collection, comprising the Lea Necklace in a simpler, more tailored version, hung with a cluster of diamond drops, and a ring and bracelet, designed as rippling diamond streams.

At the same time, the Lea Collection tapped into the ancient legends of *adamas*, evoking the myth that diamonds were tears of the gods, or splinters of the stars. Legend plays a vital role in the creation of De Beers Diamond Jewellers collections. The Swan Lake Collection is inspired by images of both water and legend from the famous ballet of that name: coloured diamonds, pink, yellow and orange, in fancy cuts, are composed into lyrical yet linear contemporary high jewellery creations, with a rhythmic harmony of shape and colour that suggests the grace of a prima ballerina. The simple, pure lines and form of the Swan Lake Collection allow the diamond to shine supreme.

Timelessness is a key aspect of the De Beers Difference, and revitalizing classic designs is an all-consuming challenge for De Beers Diamond Jewellers' design experts. Two of the most iconic, enduring forms of diamond jewellery to provide such inspiration are the solitaire and the diamond line.

The diamond line, associated with the classic 1920s line bracelet, then updated to the 'tennis' bracelet in the 1980s, is softened with the signature De Beers Diamond Jewellers femininity and fluidity. The Arpeggia Collection is designed as supple, slinky multiple strands of diamonds, playing with the idea of abundance: the abundance of nature, of femininity, of light and life. Diamonds, white, fancy and cognac-coloured, are set into micropavé mounts, so that the movement and subtle interplay of brilliance and scintillation create high drama, a moment of intense emotion generated, for example, by the sight of the sun's rays piercing a cloud, or by the thrill of a musical crescendo. The necklaces are multi-stranded, with echoes of dazzlingly bejewelled Maharajahs, while also channelling today's layered look of sophisticated, yet casual, easy couture opulence. Bracelets are slender or wide, from three to nine lines of diamonds, the earrings a single slender fluid strand or lush torrents of stones, like tassels, while the meltingly soft diamond colours are intensified by settings of white, yellow or rose-pink gold.

Line and movement are distilled into geometric forms in the Atea Collection, which revolves around the circle, a primeval symbol of eternity, of the universe and the planets, the sun and the moon. Playful, interlinked openwork circles of micropavé diamonds construct the three-dimensional designs of a pendant, earrings, ring and bracelet, all young, modern and energetic.

The solitaire finds fresh, emotive expression in collections such as the iconic Promise Ring and the Adonis Rose and Aura Collections. The Adonis Rose Solitaire Ring, a new generation engagement ring inspired by the love story of Aphrodite and Adonis, winds a leafy stem around the rose – a perfect single centre diamond. The lilting movement of the ring is exaggerated by the contrast of marquise and round brilliant diamonds. The Adonis Rose comes with a matching leafy diamond band, to fit perfectly with the engagement ring. The Aura Collection frames a single round brilliant or cushion-cut diamond with a meticulously crafted micropavé circle, creating a halo of radiant light. The centre diamond is set high, within its aura, allowing maximum light to enter the stone, while the Aura pendant and ear-studs, with an airy openwork setting, deliver vibrant variations on all-time diamond classics.

The Talisman Collection, inspired by legend, the purest expression of De Beers Diamond Jewellers design philosophy, has passed into the realm of iconic contemporary classic. Taking the diamond back to its natural state and to its earliest role as magical amulet with supernatural

Previous page, left: Untitled, a painting by Wilhelm Sasnal, 2004, courtesy of Sadie Coles HQ, London, and Hauser & Wirth, London. *Previous page, right:* Arpeggia Three-Line Necklace with 469 diamonds set in white gold, total carat weight 19.45. Arpeggia Five-Line Necklace with 722 diamonds set in white gold, total carat weight 32.02.

"Each diamond is a miracle and microcosm of nature, its perfection and chaos."

"The diamond today is a constant companion, an intimate accomplice, often worn like a second skin, day and night."

Previous page, left: Garden Bracelet in round brilliant and pear cuts, total carat weight 102.67.
Previous page, right: Artworks from the De Beers Garden Bracelet sketchbook. *Opposite: Lagoon.*
a mixed-media work by Daniel Pasteiner, 2009, courtesy of Rod Barton Gallery, London.

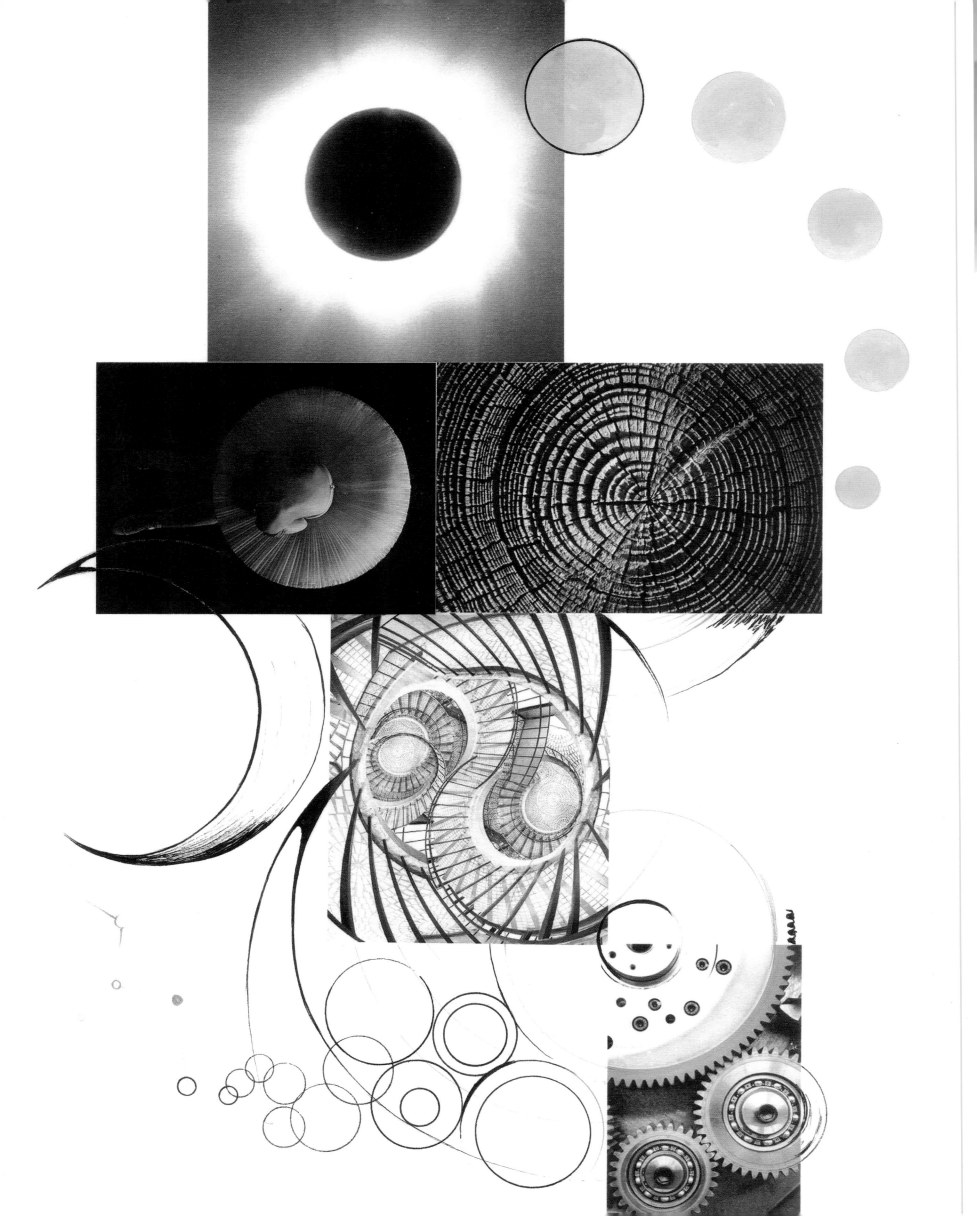

Opposite: Atea Ring with 95 diamonds set in white gold, total carat weight 0.67. Atea Sleeper Earrings with 158 diamonds set in white gold, total carat weight 1.95. Atea Small Pendant with 96 diamonds set in white gold, total carat weight 1.0. Atea Large Pendant with 205 diamonds, including a 0.30-carat centre diamond, set in white gold, total carat weight 2.45. *Previous page, left:* Mood board artworks from the De Beers Atea Collection sketchbook. *Previous page, right:* Artworks from the De Beers Atea Collection sketchbook.

"From its earliest role as magical protector, symbol of power, the diamond came to signify valour and virility, eternity, the invincibility of the soul."

"Reassuringly steadfast yet scintillating with energy, eternally modern yet reaching back to its roots as amulet and talisman, the diamond is seen as a small, intensely precious object from the depths of the earth."

Opposite: Fullmoon@Oregon Coast, a photograph by Darren Almond, 2008, courtesy of White Cube, London.

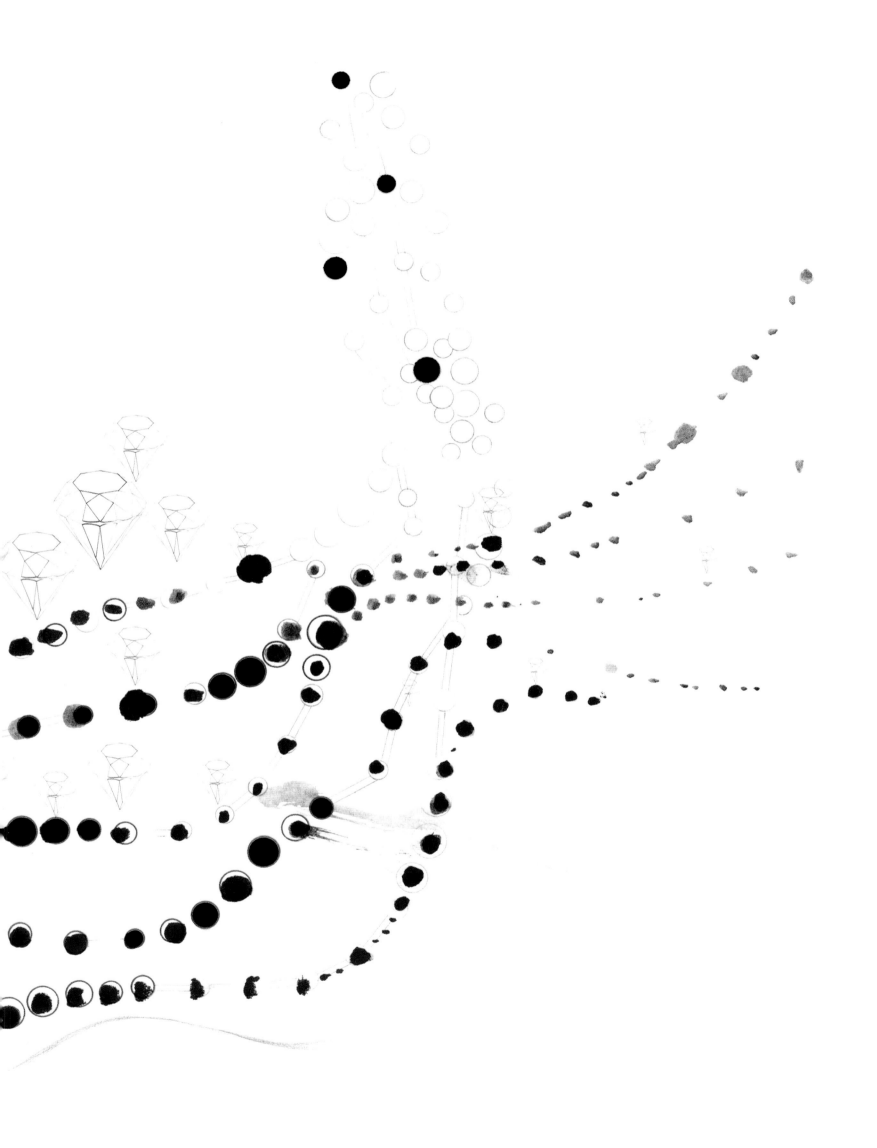

powers, an intermediary between man and otherworldly forces, the collection resonates with echoes through history, ancient to modern. Even before they were set in jewels, rough diamonds, in their natural octahedral crystalline state, were treasured for their extraordinary pyramidal form and mystical attributes. They were considered prized talismans, protective, conferring strength and victory, repelling the forces of evil, invoking good fortune. Ancient and medieval jewels, the prerogative of kings, princes and potentates, were set with rough diamonds, whose magical qualities would only be preserved if they were left in their natural state. The Talisman Collection broke with tradition to explore the mysterious charm and intense individuality of rough diamonds. It is the first contemporary collection to use rough diamonds in this way. In line with the De Beers Diamond Jewellers selection process, the rough crystals are chosen with passion and sensitivity. Andrew Coxon of the De Beers Institute of Diamonds explains: 'Naturally beautiful rough diamonds are much rarer than beautiful polished diamonds. For over 120 years, De Beers diamond experts have had the privilege of seeing many of the world's rough diamonds. Only very occasionally a naturally beautiful rough diamond of exceptional character is discovered. De Beers Diamond Jewellers is uniquely positioned to know a rare beauty when they see one'. Only one in every thousand rough diamonds is considered to have enough character, charm and beauty to win a place in a Talisman jewel.

The Talisman jewels possess a primeval sophistication, agelessly ancient and contemporary, both raw and refined. Organic, understated, yet with all the emotion and power of the diamond, the Talisman Collection has changed perceptions of diamond jewellery. When it was first launched in 2005, it struck a chord with a new generation of jewellery wearers and collectors who were looking for an entirely new, relevant and more soulful expression for this king of gemstones. Each Talisman jewel, with its distinctive, irregular, organic outline, is studded with sugary rough diamonds in subtle earth tones of brown, grey, yellow and green, their secretive sheen counterbalanced by the light of polished white diamonds.

Page 164: Arpeggia Five-Line Necklace with 722 diamonds set in white gold, total carat weight 32.02. Page 165: Musical Notes by Janaka Dharmasena. *Previous pages:* Illustration of the Arpeggia Necklace. *Opposite:* De Beers designers meticulously diagram the De Beers Talisman Wonder. *Following page, right: In Strictest Measures Even (III)* by Tatiana Echeverri Fernandez, paper collage, 2007, courtesy of Carl Freedman Gallery, London.

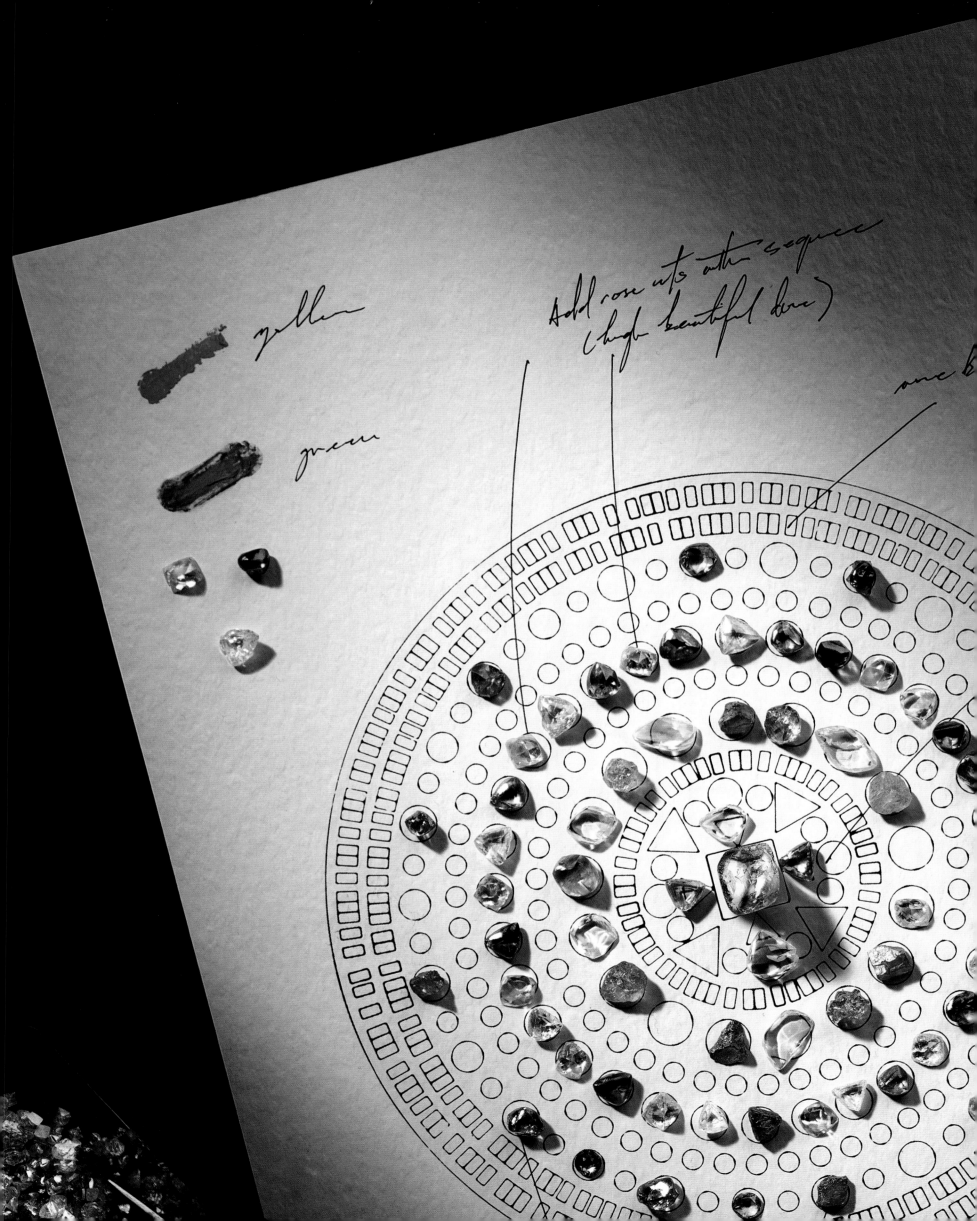

The collection has pioneered a unique setting, the *serti poincon* or 'hallmark' setting, in which hand-raised points of gold grip the diamond, lifting it above the surface, allowing light to enter but also bringing a rugged hand-hammered, ancient texture to the white and yellow gold in which the diamonds are embedded, as if growing out of a rugged rock face.

The original collection, including medallions and signet rings, has evolved into an even more sophisticated, more feminine look, with slender bands and bangles, pendants and earrings. Into the mix of rough and polished diamonds is now thrown a random scattering of rose-cut diamonds, bringing another dimension to the intriguing subtleties of luminosity and sheen. The rose is the classic antique cut, introduced in the sixteenth century and popular particularly through the eighteenth century when it sparkled flirtatiously with candlelight and intrigue.

The Talisman Wonder, revealed to the world in 2010, embodies the spirit of the Talisman Collection and the art of diamond jewellery. A unique *objet d'art*, the monumental circular gold shield or medallion is embedded with 691 diamonds, totalling 271 carats in weight, with an extraordinary centre rough diamond of over seventeen carats. The Talisman Wonder took over a year to craft in the leading Parisian workshop that creates the Talisman Collection, but its spectacular collection of diamonds – rough-coloured diamonds, rose cuts and polished white diamonds – took ten years to find and collect. The diamonds are exquisitely arranged within the distinctive hand-crafted *serti poincon* textured white gold in a mesmerising circular pattern, evocative of the most powerful, universal representations of eternity, the mandala, the universe and life force.

The Talisman Wonder was created to showcase De Beers Diamond Jewellers' dedication to natural beauty, artistry and barrier-breaking craftsmanship. In the spirit of the De Beers Millennium Star, these are masterpieces of the art of diamond jewellery, to become modern-day, timeless treasures.

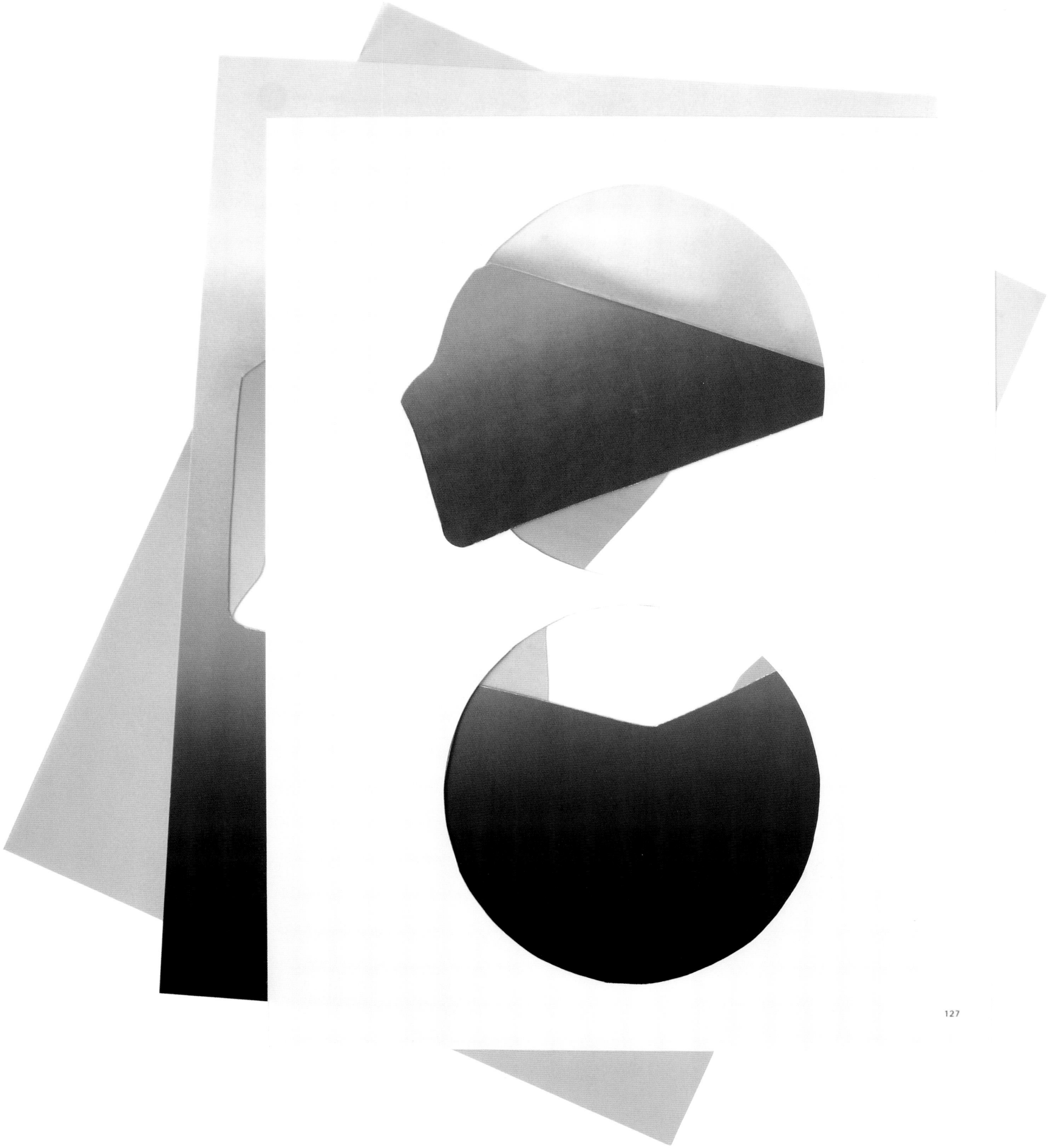

SYMBOLS

The diamond is the quintessential, universal symbol of love. From its earliest role as magical protector and symbol of power, the diamond came to signify valour and virility, eternity, the invincibility of the soul. Linked through its divine light to spiritual illumination, it represented an unbreakable bond between the owner or wearer and a higher power, the power of love. Of all its roles, the diamond as messenger of romantic love, beginning with the ancient belief that Cupid's arrows were tipped with diamonds, has resonated through the centuries. In addition to such mythical attributes, an otherworldly lustre and unbreakable strength have invested it with another layer of meaning, that of steadfast conjugal fidelity: the diamond as the physical embodiment of the most precious, everlasting bond of love and commitment.

Today, a solitaire diamond engagement ring, a symbol recognised all over the globe, continues to send its instant, unmistakable message: the ring as a circle with no beginning or end, ancient symbol of eternity, intensified by the emblematic diamond that radiates an everlasting light of love. But with the recent democratisation of the diamond, in which De Beers Diamond Jewellers plays such a vital and vibrant role, this ancient icon, whether in a ring or other jewel, has enriched its depth of meaning to become one of the most powerful symbols of personal expression – of emotion, identity, values, achievement, style, status and sentiment. It is a celebration of love and relationships of all kinds, of all of life's milestones. The diamond as love story and life story.

De Beers Diamond Jewellers has been at the forefront of dramatic changes in the perception of the diamond. One of the biggest and most significant changes, breaking a final social taboo, has been generated by women buying diamonds for themselves, thus challenging centuries-old preconceptions of the diamond as a gift from a man to a woman, the diamond as a symbol of power or 'ownership' of a woman by a man, and also breaking through barriers of age, generation and occasion. Until relatively recently, diamonds were only considered suitable for married women, or for wear after dark. Today, eons-old diamonds have become younger than ever in spirit and style, worn by all age groups, for all occasions, all day and every day, glamorously dressed up or casually sporty, from boardroom to ballroom and even the bedroom. The diamond today is a constant companion, an intimate accomplice, often worn like a second skin, day and night. Reassuringly steadfast yet scintillating, eternally modern yet reaching back to its roots as amulet and talisman, the diamond is seen as a small, intensely precious object from the depths of the earth. Linked to the spirit, it is to be kept with us at all times. De Beers Diamond Jewellers embraces this new mood with diamond jewels like the Reverie rings that celebrate occasion and personal achievement; and the Lucky Coins, modern incarnations of the amuletic associations of the diamond: the moon, a shooting star, a love letter. Self-indulgence, self-assurance.

It seems that the all-conquering diamond became linked to enduring love in the Middle Ages. A late thirteenth-century text makes reference to the diamond ring as a suitable commemoration of love and marriage, connecting the unbreakable diamond to 'unquenchable' love, stronger than death, and suggesting the ring should be worn on the ring finger, the fourth finger of the left hand, from which, according to ancient belief, a vein, the *vena amoris*, ran directly to the heart. Another thirteenth-century text stated that if a woman is incensed with her husband, relations will be soothed if she wears a diamond. This very likely still holds true today. By the fifteenth century, the diamond ring was a feature of royal and noble weddings. In 1475, Constanzo Sforza presented his bride, Camilla d'Aragona, with a diamond ring on their wedding day. The ceremony and its symbolism were recorded in a series of miniatures in a manuscript in the Vatican, along with a poem: 'Two torches in one ring of burning fire / Two wills, two hearts, two passions, all bonded in marriage by a diamond'. The ring was set with a natural rough diamond, set deep into a wide band of gold; the fire in the diamond was likened to the constant flame of love. Then, in 1477, Archduke Maximilian was advised to provide a diamond ring and a gold ring for his betrothal to Mary of Burgundy, daughter of Charles the Bold. This is generally believed to be the first recorded diamond engagement ring, a diamond intended to seal a betrothal. It was set with hogback diamonds in the form of the letter M, in celebration of

Opposite: Annabel Oval-Cut Diamond Ring, set in platinum, starting from carat weights of 2.0.

their union. In similar style, the long bar-shaped hogback diamonds could depict the *fleur-de-lis* (symbol of the Virgin Mary, suitable for a bride) or a lavish rosette as in the wedding ring of Duke Albrecht V of Bavaria. Gradually, during the Renaissance, these important rings became elaborately decorated, the diamond held high and proud in deep settings, with flourishes of enamels and richly chased shoulders and bands. Also conceived around this time, the ingenious gimmel, or twin ring, was composed of two hoops that slid open to reveal an inscription – *Whom God has joined together, let no man put asunder* – and emblematic sculptural details. Meanwhile, the intellect, word play and courtly love of the Renaissance found unusual expression when a diamond point would be used to write names or cryptic messages on windows, a favourite flirtatious pastime among nobility and royalty from Francois I of France to Elizabeth I of England.

The symbolic language of love began to flower throughout the seventeenth and eighteenth centuries, fuelled by books of emblems in which the diamond was featured for its associations with virtue, eternity and enduring lustre. The romantic gimmel ring evolved into the *fede* or faith ring, composed of clasped hands, alluding to the unity of love; the hands often clasped a diamond heart, while other rings were adorned with the flaming hearts of desire or Cupid's arrows. The seventeenth century also marked a shift away from goldsmiths' work onto the gemstone itself, and towards naturalistic designs as well as ribbons, bows, stars and arrows. Women, as well as men, wore more lavish jewellery, led by diamond-loving Queens like Marie de Medici and Anne of Austria. This culminated in the dazzling diamond splendour of the court of Louis XIV, the Sun King, who shimmered in great suites of diamonds, baubles, buttons and buckles, from head to toe. With new supplies of diamonds from Brazil, the eighteenth century, age of enlightenment, became a great age of the diamond; the effect of new and improved candlelight on diamonds, their fire newly unleashed by advanced cutting techniques, was simply dazzling. Betrothal rings, or rings with sentimental or amatory messages, became lighter and more romantic, in rococo spirit: twin hearts topped by crowns, signifying the nobility of love, or by bows and love knots, clusters of flowers in vases, love birds, or messages spelled out in diamonds. As the journey towards democratisation gathered momentum, the new wealthy merchant class, the bourgeoisie, were eager to acquire the trappings of royalty and aristocracy. The diamond was high on their list.

The association with love that was now an integral part of the diamond was fuelled by the Romantic era of the early nineteenth century, under the influence of the young Queen Victoria and her passion for sentimental jewels. She had received a simple enamel band set with a single diamond as a gift of love from Albert, before their marriage, and her own engagement ring was a serpent, an ancient symbol of protection and, with its tail in its mouth, of eternity. In the wake of the Industrial Revolution, diamonds became symbols too of status, of wealth and success, bursting into bloom in effusive, naturalistic flower sprays and voluptuous clusters. Meanwhile engagement rings, which still often incorporated symbolic motifs, such as hearts, hands and love knots, became more substantial as the century progressed, developing into recognisable modern styles: the half-hoop of diamonds on an engraved gold shank, the three-diamond ring, the 'gypsy' setting, in which the diamonds are set into the gold band, their surfaces level with the gold, sometimes embedded in a star setting.

The Belle Époque, the Edwardian era and America's Gilded Age with their tycoons, industrialists, bankers and socialites, the dashing jewel-bedecked Maharajahs and exotic Sultans, and the new supply of jewels from South Africa, all conspired to usher in another truly great age of the diamond. At a time of enormous wealth and leisured luxury, the indomitable king of gemstones, with its layers of legend, was lusted after as the ultimate possession, the quintessential symbol of power. For the great courtesans and actresses of the day, the *grandes horizontales*, as they were known, diamonds were the currency of love: public, tangible signifiers of their secret successes and, more prosaically, their security; they engaged in fierce competition over the size and value of their jewel boxes. In more respectable circles, the engagement ring, so often sealing strategic alliances of great wealth with social stature, was focused very much on a significant single diamond, now in its classic open-prong setting, showing its new brilliance to perfection.

Following pages: Selection of artworks from the De Beers Solitaire sketchbooks.

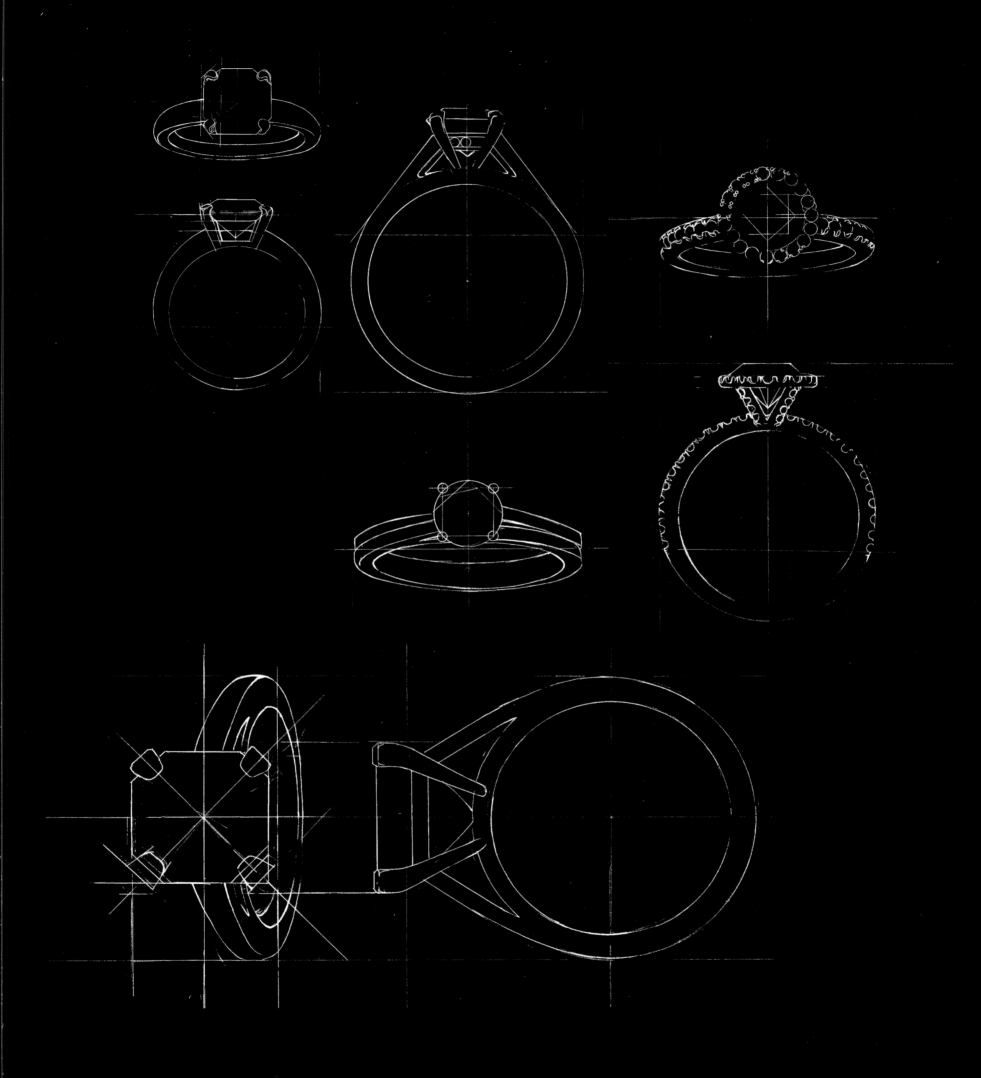

De Beers Diamond Jewellers honours this long and illustrious tradition and at the same time takes the engagement ring into the future, in new directions, with lightness, movement and meaning, understanding that this is likely to be one of the most important jewels of a woman's life – often her first seriously precious jewel and a ring to be worn all day, every day. Their aim is to deliver a diamond that goes way beyond a client's hopes and expectations in terms of quality, brilliance and visual excitement. Next, they ensure the diamond can be viewed clearly from all sides, that it sits high in its setting to catch maximum light, with a minimum of metal surrounding it, so that it shines supreme. The Promise Ring, the iconic De Beers engagement ring, entwines a slender platinum band with a diamond band – two lovers uniting – that together enclose a single diamond. The Adonis Rose, a composition of twisting leaves and a soft petalled rose in which nestles a single diamond, digs deep into antiquity and pays homage to Aphrodite, goddess of love. Both are complemented by matching diamond-set wedding bands. The Eternity Ring, also a band of diamonds, is transformed at De Beers Diamond Jewellers into a contemporary gift of love, often commemorating a wedding anniversary or the birth of a child. The Match Bands are slender micropavé-set bands of white, pink or yellow diamonds, perfect for a wedding or eternity ring, worn one at a time or stacked together.

It was in the Belle Époque, with its cult of femininity, that the diamond began its journey through the twentieth century. Enveloped in the art of seduction as epitomised by Marilyn Monroe, who made diamonds forever a girl's best friend, and encapsulated by the magnificent Taylor-Burton diamond and other diamond jewels that charted tempestuous love affairs, diamonds emerge, glittering, in the twenty-first century as the most powerful expression of the eternal feminine.

Opposite, from top: Butterfly Ring from De Beers Reverie Collection with 70 white round brilliant diamonds set in 18K white gold, total carat weight 0.80; Channel Set Full Eternity Band with white round brilliant diamonds set in platinum, total carat weight for standard size 0.58; Pavé Swan Band from the Reverie Collection, with 168 white round brilliant diamonds set in 18K white gold, total carat weight 1.30; Darling Pavé Eternity Band from the Reverie Collection, with round brilliant micropavé diamonds set in 18K white gold, total carat weight for standard size 1.10; Pink, White and Yellow Petal Bands from the De Beers Reverie Collection with sixteen pear-cut and round brilliant diamonds set in pink, white and yellow gold, total carat weight 0.70; Dewdrop Ring from De Beers Reverie Collection with 112 diamonds set in 18K white gold, total carat weight 1.00; Full Eternity Band with 0.40-carat round brilliant diamonds set in platinum; Pink and White Gold Match Bands from De Beers Reverie Collection with white round brilliant micropavé diamonds set in pink and white gold, total carat weight for standard size 0.35; Yellow Gold Match Band from De Beers Reverie Collection with yellow round brilliant micropavé diamonds set in yellow gold, total carat weight for standard size 0.35; Enchanted Lotus Band from De Beers Enchanted Lotus Collection with white round brilliant diamonds set in 18K white gold, total carat weight 1.05; Channel Set Full Eternity Band, with white round brilliant diamonds set in platinum, total carat weight for standard size 2.18.

Opposite: Wildflowers, a photograph of London by Ori Gersht, 2005. *Following pages:* Selection of artworks from the De Beers Reverie Collection sketchbooks.

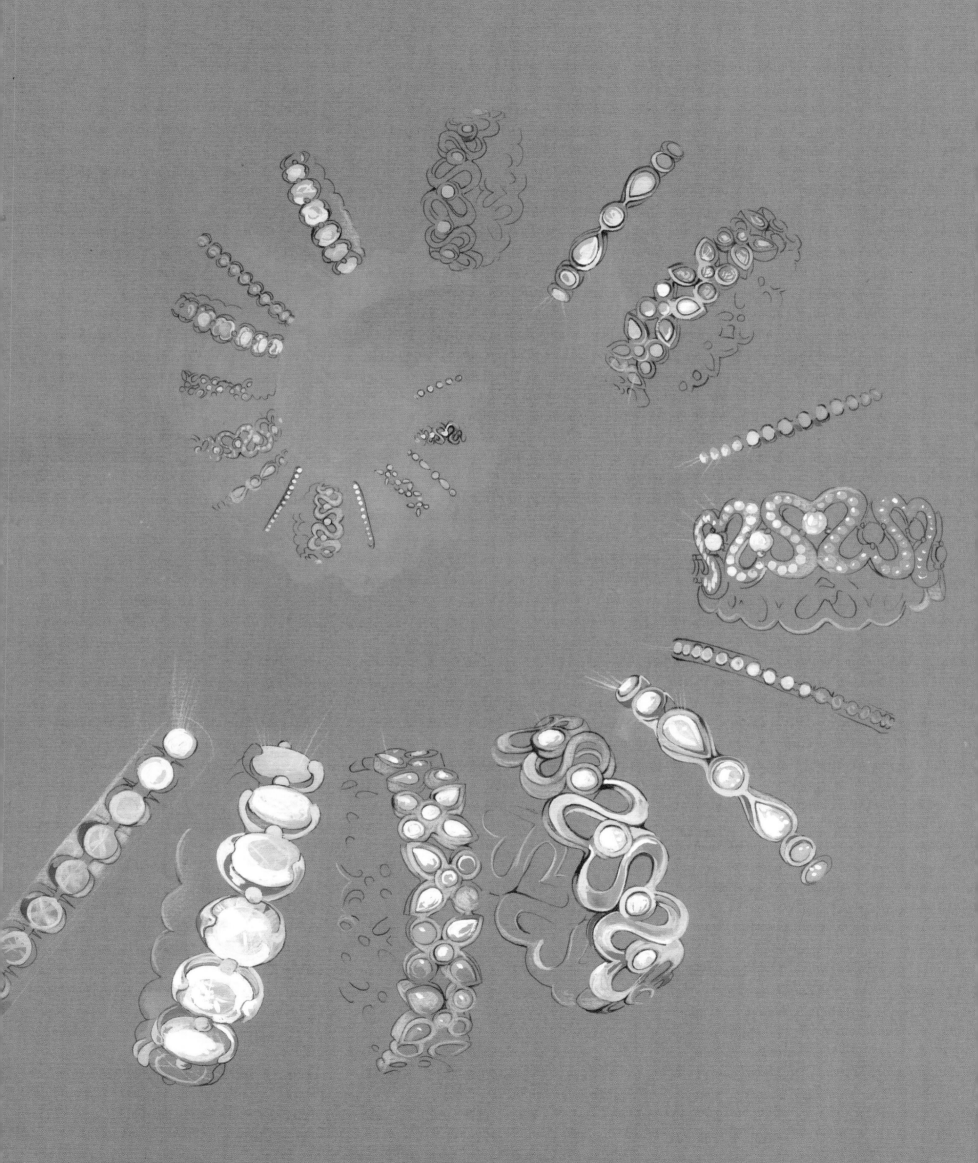

The early nineties, years of grunge-inspired non-adornment, turned out to be the decorative lull before the storm: as the mood changed, supermodels seized on diamonds, pure, iconic and real, the essence of minimal-with-meaning, to bring ornamentation back in a fresh way. After the surfeit of the eighties, the new generation loved the cool simplicity of single diamonds, stud earrings, the iconic diamond cross. The young elitocracy saw the diamond as a vehicle for rebellion against established rules. They bought their own diamonds, wearing them, subversively, for daytime, with sportswear, in clubs, in the hair, irreverently. They all discovered an undeniable and unchanging truth: there is an ageless chemistry between women and diamonds; diamonds make women look and feel good; diamonds cut through styles and across generations. De Beers Diamond Jewellers was quick to pick up on the change in attitude, combining deep respect for the long heritage of the diamond with fresh, iconoclastic innovation.

A new mood of luxury – young, accessible, authentic – settled over the new millennium as De Beers Diamond Jewellers began a new chapter of diamond jewellery, fanning the flames of diamond desire in the process. Women refused to wait to be given diamonds; they wanted to take control, to wear them as trophies of their own self-respect and achievement. A well-deserved treat; their birthright.

Women today are discerning, well-informed diamond connoisseurs. Even when diamonds are a gift from a man, the woman is involved in the purchase. A woman looks for a diamond jewel that fits her multifaceted roles and personal style; one that captures *l'air du temps*; one that's design-driven yet beyond fashion. Over the past decade, in a process of feminisation, women have subtly yet powerfully influenced design, nurturing ingenuity and audacity, introducing lightness, fluidity, wit and storytelling. There is an intimacy in today's diamond with the body; it has to feel good on the skin, and be light, fluid, tactile, sensual. Today the diamond remains the powerful universal symbol it has always been, of love, luck, protection and celebration, of romance and adventure, but also a symbol of freedom, fantasy and femininity.

" Taking the diamond back to its natural state and to its earliest role as magical amulet with supernatural powers, an intermediary between man and otherworldly forces, the Talisman Collection resonates with echoes through history, ancient to modern. "

" A symbol of freedom, fantasy and femininity.
Of pride in achievement, self-esteem, self-respect.
The diamond as eternal love token, trophy and talisman.
The divine diamond and the power of love. "

Previous page, right: Cave (Ir.T n° 513), a mixed-media work by Ibon Aranberri, 2003. *Opposite:* Talisman Medallion in rough, rose and round brilliant cuts set in yellow gold, total carat weight 1.91. *Following page, left: Paris Couple*, a photograph by Frank Horvat, 1955. *Page 192:* De Beers Aura Ring with radiant-cut fancy intense yellow diamond, total carat weight approximately 4.0. DB Classic Solitaire with round brilliant-cut diamond, colour G, clarity VS1, set with tapered baguettes, total carat weight 8.82. DB Classic Solitaire with Asscher-cut diamond set on a simple shank, carat weight approximately 6 carats.

ACKNOWLEDGMENTS

We would like to thank the following artists, galleries and organisations for their assistance and collaboration on this project:

De Beers Group; De Beers Group Archives; Chris Alderman; Darren Almond; Ibon Aranberri; Coppi Barbieri; Hollie Bonneville Barden; Paul Barry; Rod Barton Gallery, London; Beinecke Rare Book and Manuscript Library, Yale University; Malin Bergström; India/Dinodia/The Bridgeman Art Library; Paul Calver; Rob and Nick Carter; Contemporary Fine Arts, Berlin; Sadie Coles HQ, London; Andrew Coxon; Robert Diament; Luke Dowd; Tatiana Echeverri Fernandez; The Field Museum; Fine Art Society, London; Richard Foster; Carl Freedman Gallery, London; Ori Gersht; Charles Gute; Hauser & Wirth, London; Kim Hersov; Sarah Jones; Christina K; Barbara Kasten; Hirst Holdings Limited and Damien Hirst; Euan MacGregor; Michael Marcelle; Maureen Paley, London; Daniel Pasteiner; Wilhelm Sasnal; Tal R; Wolfgang Tillmans; Nils-Udo; David Watling; James Welling; White Cube, London; and Joe Wilson. Thanks also to the Assouline Publishing team.

All text except the foreword written by Vivienne Becker, 2010.